The Practice of Homefulness

the practice of
HOMEFULNESS

Walter Brueggemann

EDITED BY
K. C. Hanson

CASCADE *Books* · Eugene, Oregon

THE PRACTICE OF HOMEFULNESS

Cascade Books
An Imprint of Wipf and Stock Publishers
199 W. 8th Ave., Suite 3
Eugene, OR 97401

www.wipfandstock.com

ISBN 13: 978-1-62564-588-3

Cataloging-in-Publication data:

Brueggemann, Walter.

   The practice of homefulness / Walter Brueggemann ; edited and with a
Foreword by K. C. Hanson.

   xii + 106 p.; 21.5 cm. Includes bibliographical references and indexes.

   ISBN 13: 978-1-62564-588-3

   1. Preaching. 2. Bible. O.T.—Homiletical use. I. Hanson, K. C. (Kenneth
C.). II. Title.

BS1191.5 B75 2014

Manufactured in the U.S.A.

Contents

Foreword

I am not sure what metaphors Walter Brueggemann would choose to describe his role as biblical exegete. Explorer? Guide? Excavator? He is surely all of these. But the one that comes to my mind is *fascilitator*.

He brings his considerable skills to bear on the text as a rhetorical critic, linguist, historian, social critic, and theologian. But ulltimately and foremost he fascilitates the conversation between the biblical text and his audience. His attention to the details, metaphors, sequences, relationships, tensions, emotions, gaps, social dimensions, and theological foci in a passage fascilitate our understanding of—and then further conversation with—the biblical writers and their messages. To use Clifford Geertz's well-known phrase, Walter drives toward "thick description." Ultimately that thick description brings us into conversation with God. He keeps that centuries-long conversation going.

He also fascilitates that conversation by bringing different biblical voices into conversation with one another. How does what Deutero-Isaiah was saying at the end of the exilic period relate to what Trito-Isaiah was saying during the post-exilic period? How does Amos's bold call for justice relate to the behavior of the monarchy and the urban elites described in the books of Samuel and Kings? How do the diverse images of David in the books of Samuel, Psalms, and Chronicles relate to one another? How do the cries of the oppressed, the dispirited, the sick, and the dying relate to the praise of the creator?

And he fascilitates the conversation between the biblical text and our contemporary situation. He exposes the treacheries of empire, triumphalism, and commodification of virtually everything. But his goal is not some sort of simplistic finger-pointing or scolding. Like the ancient Israelite and Judean prophets, his goal is to help us to see what is really going on beneath the surface. To shake us from our complacency. To alert us to the abuses of power. To enliven us to new possibilities. To unmask political rhetoric, intensive marketing, and media bombardment. To help us discover alternatives—alternative voices, alternative communities, alternative strategies.

The essays in this volume follow the earlier volumes collecting articles from the *Journal of Preachers*: *Truth-telling as Subversive Obedience* (2011), *Remember You Are Dust* (2012), and *Embracing the Transformation* (2014).

K. C. Hanson
Ash Wednesday 2014

Preface

The span of these essays reflects my thinking over several years, but I believe that the accent points in what I have written continue to be current and urgent. I am yet again grateful to my colleague, Erskine Clarke, for his willingness to have republished these articles that I have written over time for the *Journal for Preachers*, which he edits.

Jeremiah 22:15–16 continues to be a pivot point in my thinking wherein "care for the poor and needy" is equated by the prophet with "knowledge of Yahweh." That is, Yahweh is known in and through the praxis of faith that refuses to separate thought from action, body from spirit, or earth from heaven. This characteristic insistence of biblical faith is so urgent in the church precisely because the church continues to be tempted by a kind of transcendentalism that removes the will and purpose of God from the "mundane" matters of economics and politics. It is exactly that dualism that so pervades modern thought against which the Old Testament bears such powerful witness.

The accent on *praxis*, on the actual concrete bodily performance of faith, that is, performance of Yahweh, is related to two other themes in this modest collection. The theme of "homefulness" stresses both being with and belonging with God and being with and belonging with the neighbor in community. But transcendental thought that separates faith from public life eventuates in an unregulated privatism that subverts community and renders the "unproductive" as acutely vulnerable. The end result of such transcendental thought via privatism is the production of homelessness wherein the "unproductive" are denied, by an economics of greed and the politics of oligarchy, a viable place in society. We live in a political economy, expressed as individualism and legitimated by transcendental theology, that is not only inhospitable to the homeless, but in fact is productive of home-lessness. And of course that homelessness at hand stands as a sign and reminder of the refugee-producing policies enacted world-wide by the hand of unrestrained violent power. A focus on homelessness is for that reason urgent, because faith refuses to allow that some should be abandoned "widows and orphans." Homelessness, as with every theme in the Bible, pertains at the same time to at-homeness with God and at-homeness with the neighbor.

Given the production of homelessness, a second theme in the present collection is pivotal, namely, forgiveness. It is only forgive-ness that may break the vicious cycle of greedy anxiety that issues in violence, often "legal" violence. Forgiveness in biblical faith runs the spectrum from forgiveness of sins before God to forgiveness of debt concerning the neighbor. It is exactly the *praxis* of Yahweh that performs the work of Yahweh who,

> forgives all your iniquity,
>> who heals all your diseases,
> who delivers your life from the Pit,
>> who crowns you with steadfast love and mercy,
> who satisfies you with good as long as you live,
>> so that your youth is renewed like the eagle's. (Ps 103:3–5)

That God "will not keep his anger forever" (Ps 103:9) is deeply re-lated to the social practice of the "year of release" (Deut 15:1–18) and the Year of Jubilee (Leviticus 25), both proposals and that would "not keep debt forever." That is, by the mercy of God there is a statue of limitation on divine anger and on human debt. The practice of forgiveness runs all the way from welcoming back into the family those who are disqualified (as in Luke 15) to welcoming back the "unproductive" into the economy in a viable way.

For all the ready criticism of the South African Truth and Rec-onciliation Commission, that dramatic process stands as an instance of a society facing into the "not keeping anger forever," and engag-ing in forgiveness that may permit some people to "return home." The process was inescapably flawed, but it stands, nonetheless, as testimony to what is socially possible when the "other" is seen in human terms.

Of the learnings about forgiveness that emerged from the process of "Truth and Reconciliation," Desmond Tutu and his daughter, Mpho, have concluded:

> When I develop a mindset of forgiveness, rather than a mindset of grievance, I don't just forgive a particular act; I become a more forgiving person. With a grievance mindset, I look at the world and see all that is wrong. When I have a forgiveness mindset, I start to see the world not through grievance but through gratitude. In other words, I look at the world and start to see what is right. There is a special kind of magic that happens when I become a more forgiving person—it is something quite remarkable. What was once a grave affront melts into nothing more than a thoughtless or careless act. What was once a reason for rupture and alienation becomes an opportunity for repair and greater intimacy. A life that seemed littered with obstacles and antagonism is suddenly filled opportunity and love.[1]

In her review of the work of the Truth and Reconciliation Commission, Catherine Cole has especially appreciated the fact that the process of forgiveness had to be dramatically performed so that all could see, and so that the process of forgiveness was not an idea but an inescapable social fact. In her review of the performance of the Commission, none of the testimony that she cites is more poignant than that of Nomonde Calata, wife of the murdered activist Fort Calata. Concerning the testimony of Calata, Cole quotes the words of a commissioner and of Antjie Krog, who has written of that testimony. Cole writes:

> Calata's wail "shook the very foundation of the hall. She flung her head back in desolation. I cannot forget that cry". . . "For me, this crying is the beginning of the Truth Commission—the signature tune, the definitive moment, the ultimate sound of what the process is about. She was wearing this vivid orange-red dress, and she

---

1. Tutu and Tutu, *The Book of Forgiving*, 218–19.

threw herself backward and that sound . . . that sound
. . . it will haunt me for ever and ever" . . . When I asked
her how she felt about her cry becoming an iconic moment of the commission . . . she answered, "That is why
I screamed—because I wanted the pain to come out. I
was tired of keeping it inside me because even the time
when my husband died, people would not allow me to
cry because I was expecting a baby, so they were thinking that my crying would affect the baby. So I never had
enough time to cry."[2]

My thinking has of course moved on from these essays. But K.
C. Hanson has nicely seen a convergence of themes in this collection.
The urgency of practice, the cruelty of homelessness and the demand
of generating homefulness, and the performance of forgiveness that
makes homefulness possible all converge. These themes, moreover,
are unmistakably contemporary in a society that is mesmerized by
market ideology that wants religion without public practice, that sees
no harm in the homelessness of the "unproductive," and that eschews
the forgiveness of debt that make neighborly life possible. I am glad if
these essays bear testimony to the crisis we continue face and to the
work to which we are continually called in faith.

I am especially grateful to K. C. Hanson and to his companions
at Wipf and Stock for initiating this collection and seeing it through.
K. C. brings to such work both energy and imagination that make
the best and the most of what I have tried to do in these essays. My
work consists mainly in reading texts. And the texts keep showing up
among us with transformative and summoning power.

Walter Brueggemann
Christmas week, 2013

2. Cole, *Performing South Africa's Truth Commission*, 79.

I

The Practice of Homefulness

It is my conviction that learning to reread the Bible is not only enormously interesting, but enormously urgent, for in rereading the Bible, we will be permitted to reread our social reality. This double rereading is important, I believe, because what we need in relation to this problem of homelessness is not information, but courage, energy, will, freedom, and impetus. And those permits will come, not from socioeconomic, political analysis, important as such analysis is, but from our deepest texts where we hear a voice of holiness that can intrude upon our settled sense of self and our settled social reality.

The preacher has an important opportunity to connect the problem of *homelessness* (which is much on our minds) with texts on *homefulness* as willed by *God*. Preaching is so urgent because the homelessness generated by our economy can be resituated in a context of evangelical homefulness. I will consider a series of texts and then draw some conclusions. I have as a very modest goal that we together might see one or two texts differently, and thereby see one piece of our crisis differently.

Return to Yahweh

My first text, on which I will dwell at some length, is a throwaway line in Hos 14:1–3. Verses 1–3 are a final invitation in the book of Hosea to repent:

> Return, O Israel, to Yahweh your God,
>> for you have stumbled because of your iniquity.
> Take words with you and return to Yahweh;
>> say to him, "Take away all guilt;
> Accept that which is good, and we will offer
>> the fruit of our lips.
> Assyria will not save us; we will not ride upon horses;
>> we will say no more, 'Our God,' to the work of our hands.
> In you the orphan finds mercy."

"Return to Yahweh." That's the first line, reiterated in the second verse. The following verses answer the question, return from what?:

- return from iniquity, for you have stumbled into *false faith;*

- return from wrong speech, where you have embraced *self-deceptive ideology,*

- return from horses and Assyrians, *mistaken security* in arms,

- return from the work of our hands, *self-sufficiency.*

That is a lot to give up: false faith, false ideology, mistaken security, self-sufficiency.

As is usual in Hebrew poetry, the last line circles back on the first line. Notice, nothing yet has been said to characterize Yahweh, the one to whom return is to be made. What would it mean to return to Yahweh? Then comes the punch line, the most important line: "In you, the orphan finds mercy!" What a line! Critical scholarship says it is a late gloss in the poem.[1] But there it is. The statement has three phrases. *In you,* in the God of Israel, the liberator of slaves, the giver of commandments, the patron of covenant, the provider of land. "In you" recalls and makes present the entire long history of Yahweh, the history of the only God who cares about land, food, clothing, houses, material well-being.

The second phrase is *the orphan.* Remember, this text comes out of a tribal society with large, extended families with inheritance, genealogy, pedigree, and patrimony. It is a society in which everyone has a place and belongs, and is known there and named and cared

---

1. See, for example, Wolff, *Hosea,* 231–32. But against such a tendency, see Andersen and Freedman, *Hosea,* 645–46.

for...unless your daddy has died. The problem about being an orphan is not that you grieve over your dead daddy. It is rather that you lose your place. If your daddy died, you do not belong, you are without name, genealogy, pedigree, patrimony, defense, rescue, advocate, avenger. You are always, everywhere at risk and in jeopardy. That is how the world was ordered in the olden days. And if we reflect long, we see that the realities of social power have not changed much. It is a high risk deal to have lost your place in the tribal world.

Thus in the first two phrases of this poetic line, we have an odd juxtaposition. There is Yahweh who has this long, faithful history of intervention and provision, and there is the orphan, who has no name, no history, no prospect, no chance in the world. Yahweh is the guarantor, the orphan is the one who has no guarantees.

Everything hinges on the third term of the poetic line, find mercy. It is in mercy that the guarantor and the one without guarantees get together. The two are linked in mercy, the mercy that comes from Yahweh and goes to the orphan. The term "mercy" denotes womb-like mother love, massive attentiveness and solidarity, fidelity that cuts underneath merit to give guarantees.[2] This is the one who gives guarantees for life to the one who has no guarantees for life. Thus, the entire rhetorical unit says, a) leave off false faith, false ideology, mistaken security, and self-sufficiency; b) get back in obedience to the one who gives guarantees to those who lack every guarantee. I suspect that this text will do for us both because of its powerful witness to God, and because it is precisely such foundational repentance that is required, if we are to have any serious housing revolution.

This marvelous text, however, is open to an insidious and mistaken reading. I take "mercy to the orphan" to be a fairly precise equivalent to "homes for the homeless," because the homeless are the genuine orphans in our society, for they have no protective tribe. In such a context, "mercy" translates into "a house," which bespeaks membership in a protective community.

The danger for interpretation is that mercy for the orphan, homes for the homeless, comes from Yahweh. It is entirely possible, even if dead wrong, to take the text as an invitation to quiescence and abdication, to conclude that God gives mercy to orphans, and

---

2. See Trible, *God and the Rhetoric of Sexuality*, 31–59.

if God gives homes to the homeless, then homelessness is settled, overcome, and not our problem. And of course with a bad theology of otherworldliness, the church has often invited such a reading. When the Bible is read so transcendentally, then the human dimension of the housing crisis is cut off from our theological confession, and only knee jerk liberals sign on, and often they are without energy or durability.

It is for that reason that we must work at serious rereading of the Bible away from our transcendental naivete. I suggest that while mercy and orphan are clear enough in their meanings, what we have to work on for this verse is "in you," "in Yahweh," the one to whom we are summoned to return. A number of scholars—especially Norman Gottwald, but also Robert Coote, Marvin Chaney, and Frank Frick—have derived from the character of Yahweh a central insight of serious social criticism.[3] That key insight is that in terms of cultural linguistics, "God talk" is never transcendental, spiritual, and otherworldly, but it always carries within it, willy-nilly, an implicit and tacit theory of social relations. That is, "God talk" is inherently laden with socioeconomic and political implications. This is, so I argue thus far, simply a formal claim of all religious talk.

When we push beyond formal to substantive matters about the Bible, however, we are not interested in a theoretical notion of "God talk," but now focus more precisely of "Yahweh talk." Thus when Hosea says "Return to Yahweh your God" and concludes by saying "in you," what is being said? The answer I propose is that in Mosaic-prophetic faith it belongs undeniably to the very character of Yahweh—of Yahwism—to foster, advocate, and enact a certain social practice. That is, Yahweh is not a God safely in heaven or in church, but Yahweh is in fact a *specific social practice* which is taken seriously in obedient Israel. When one "returns to Yahweh," one must return to the social practice in which Yahweh, Yahweh's people, Yahweh's community, and Yahweh's covenant are definitionally involved.

To this I add a supporting text from Jeremiah, who learned so much from Hosea. Speaking of good kings and bad kings, and offering King Josiah as a model for a good king, the poet asserts:

3. See, for example, Gottwald, *The Tribes of Yahweh*; Gottwald, ed., *Social Scientific Criticism of the Hebrew Bible and Its Social World: The Israelite Monarchy*; and Frick, *The Formation of the State in Ancient Israel*.

> He judged the cause of the poor and needy;
>> then it was well.
> Is not this to know me?
>> says Yahweh. (Jer 22:16)

This is an extraordinary text which shows how Yahweh is understood in terms of social practice.[4] Note well, the text does not say: if one takes care of the poor and the needy, then that one will get to know Yahweh. Nor does the text say: if one knows Yahweh, then one will take care of the poor and needy. The two elements are not sequential nor are they related as cause and effect. Rather the two phrases are synonymous. *Caring for the poor and needy* is equivalent to *knowing Yahweh*. That is who Yahweh is and how Yahweh is known. Yahweh is indeed a mode of social practice and a way of social relation.

Thus Jer 22:16 illuminates Hos 14:1–3. "Return to Yahweh" means to return to the God who is present in social practice that is a sharp contrast to false faith, false ideology, mistaken security, and self-sufficiency. The housing crisis among the orphans will not be solved by turning things over to a holy God in heaven, nor by heroic action on our part, but by increasing investment in the social practice wherein Yahweh is present, a social practice that in every generation and every circumstance involves liberation and covenant, gifts and land.[5] Notice that this social practice wherein Yahweh is known and visible characteristically and inevitably clashes with the *status quo* and evokes big time displacement of present power, money, and housing arrangements. Thus the housing problem, when construed evangelically, that is, according to the gospel, is an evangelical task, inviting more folks into the story and social practice defined by the character of this God. It is no stretch of rhetoric to conclude that such a "return to Yahweh" brings together our baptism, that is, embrace of the gospel, and the concrete practice of Yahweh in giving guarantees to orphans. The prophetic alternative is always aimed against a split between the transcendence of God and the social practice of God, that is, between word and flesh.

4. See the discussion of this text by Miranda, *Marx and the Bible*, 47–72.

5. See Brueggemann, *The Land*.

Yahweh's Story of Housing

Now with this framing program, "In you, the orphan finds mercy," I thought it would be most useful to lay out a taxonomy of Yahweh's story of housing. This consists, as I understand the assignment, of calling attention to some crucial texts and suggesting how they may be linked together in a coherent and authorizing sequence. I shall do so in three groups that correspond to the three seasons of the life of ancient Israel. The first season includes three texts that reflect on *the originary claim of having a house*. At the outset Israel assumes all of Yahweh's people will indeed have a home.

Deuteronomy 6:10–13

> When Yahweh our God has brought you into the land that he swore to your ancestors, to Abraham, to Isaac, and to Jacob, to give you—a land with fine, large cities that you did not build, houses filled with all sorts of goods that you did not fill, hewn cisterns that you did not hew, vineyards and olive groves that you did not plant—and when you have eaten your fill, take care that you do not forget Yahweh, who brought you out of the land of Egypt, out of the house of slavery. Yahweh your God you shall fear; him you shall serve, and by his name alone you shall swear.

This old account of houses in ancient Israel acknowledges that houses are a free, unearned, inexplicable gift. This uncommon conviction makes sense when we remember that the earliest theological vision and memory in Israel came out of marginal, disadvantaged peasants who were exploited and marginalized.[6] They had no secure home and no prospect of a secure home. They lived at the whim of the managers of the economy and were endlessly in jeopardy. Then there occurred, abruptly, a theological revolution in the world. Yahweh

---

6. It is, of course, the case that the refraction of that early vision in the tradition of Deuteronomy is formulated much later. Nonetheless, the passions which drive the tradition are surely rooted in the faith and social experience of the very origins of Israel. On critical questions related to the tradition of Deuteronomy, see Miller, *Deuteronomy*.

began to notice and to care and to move. Or as Gottwald prefers, this was a Yahweh-authorized sociopolitical revolution whereby the citadels of monopoly were burned to the ground and goods were made available, which only recently had appeared well beyond any reach or any hope.[7] Peasants who dared never dream came into unexpected prosperity and security. The text calls this "the triumphs of the Yahweh, the triumphs of his peasantry in Israel" (Judg 5:11). What could the peasants say except "Thanks," uttered with awe and gratitude. That is the beginning of a housing horizon in ancient Israel, "houses you did not fill," utter gift.

This newly given property is pervasively a covenantal arrangement. The ones who occupy the land and inhabit the houses are bound to the generous giver: "Him you shall fear, you shall serve, you shall swear by." The house is a gift only in the relation. Notice that Yahweh is now redefined by houses freely given. Houses are likewise redefined by Yahwistic command. Houses are placed irreversibly in the context of covenant, that is, in the context of an alternative social vision and an alternative social requirement. The temptation of Israel is to have houses without Yahweh, and Yahweh without houses, but Deuteronomy will tolerate no retreat from covenantal definitions of social reality. Israel dare not forget, but must remember the strange gift of houses in a world where none seemed available. It is in the form of a house that this orphan people found mercy.

Psalm 112

Praise Yah!
How honorable are those who fear Yahweh,
    who greatly delight in his commandments.
Their descendants will be mighty in the land;
    the generation of the upright will be blessed.

---

7. I am following the hypothesis of a "peasant revolt" proposed by George E. Mendenhall and carefully pursued by Norman Gottwald. That hypothesis makes the most sense out of the violent destructions through which the promises of God were fulfilled to land-hungry Israel. See my discussion of that violence in Brueggemann, *Divine Presence amid Violence*.

Wealth and riches are in their houses,
and their righteousness endures forever.
They rise in the darkness as a light for the upright;
they are gracious, merciful, and righteous.
It is well with those who deal generously and lend,
who conduct their affairs with justice.
For the righteous will never be moved;
they will be remembered forever.
They are not afraid of evil tidings;
their heart is firm, secure in the Lord.
Their hearts are steady, they will not be afraid;
in the end they will look in triumph on their foes.
They have distributed freely,
they have given to the poor;
Their righteousness endures forever;
their horn is exalted in honor.
The wicked see it and are angry;
they gnash their teeth and melt away;
The desire of the wicked comes to nothing.

The tradition of Deuteronomy is a tradition of unmerited gift: "It was not because you were more numerous . . ." (Deut 7:7). "It was not because of my righteousness . . ." (Deut 9:4–5).

There is, however, a second opinion in the Bible about how one comes into possession of a house. Whereas the first tradition (Deuteronomy) arises out of a community of peasants who were surprised at having a house, this second tradition sounds like the voice of those well situated, who take their adequate housing as their proper claim and entitlement.[8] I call this a tradition of "self-congratulatory righteousness." It reflects the sentiment of those who believe that their material situation of prosperity is their right and their achievement, their reward for services rendered.

Thus Psalm 112 is an observation concerning the ones who fear God and keep commandments and who consequently are "mighty in

8. Guthrie, *Theology as Thanksgiving*, 19–21, has nicely suggested a correlation between social setting and liturgical voicing.

the land." Their houses are filled with wealth and riches, and they are unendingly righteous.[9] They practice justice and are "never moved," that is, never destabilized or placed in jeopardy. They are endlessly steady, secure, stable, generous, and are the envy of the others. People who have secure houses find it persuasive to imagine a stable, well-ordered moral universe where good people are housed and others gnash their teeth and melt away.

This psalm of self-congratulations is echoed by Psalm 37, a meditation on how righteousness yields much prosperity, that is, land. In one of the most unseemly statements in the Bible, the psalmist asserts:

> I have been young, and now I am old,
>> yet I have not seen the righteous forsaken
>> or their children begging for bread.
> They are ever giving liberally and lending,
>> and their children become a blessing. (Ps 37:25–26)

In a long life of observation of society, the speaker has never seen any righteous person reduced to poverty, nor their children reduced to begging. It is a simple interpretive maneuver to conclude that when one is reduced to poverty or one's children beg for bread, they are the wicked, that is, the undeserving poor.

Admittedly, I have cited two extreme cases. But they are important because they help form the limits of the difficult conversation in the Bible about housing. The two views in Deuteronomy and the Psalms I have cited are socially conditioned, reflecting the experience of the surprisingly housed and the complacently housed. These two views run throughout scripture and into our own time. They pose the question of how access to housing is to be discerned in a convenantal world where God makes and keeps promises, where God issues commands, and where God invites obedience and grants rewards.

When Yahweh is social practice as well as sovereign Lord, it makes an enormous difference if there are houses freely given out of God's abundance, or if houses are only a pay-out for a certain kind of socially approved conduct, that is, whether house is gift or pay-out.

---

9. See the same claims of well-being for the righteous in Job 21:7–16, only now uttered ironically and polemically.

Deuteronomy 10:12–22

I cite one other text that I would place at the point of origin in the biblical discussion of housing. This remarkable text voices at the same time the largest vision of Yahweh's sovereignty, and the most concrete ethical demand God can utter. On the one hand, this is the one who is "God of gods, Lord of lords, mighty and awesome" (v. 17). On the other hand, this is the God "who takes no bribes, who executes justice for orphans and widows, and who loves strangers" (vv. 17b–18a) Indeed, this God is at work providing food and clothing for disenfranchised people (v. 18b). This is, to be sure, doxological language; but even in doxological language, it is clear that the Lord of lords and God of gods does not give food and clothing to vulnerable outsiders by supernaturalist fiat, but by social practice.

Our point of interest in this text, however, is not in the indicative doxology, but in the derivative imperative:

> You shall also love the stranger,
>
> for you were strangers in the land of Egypt. (v. 19)[10]

This is an extraordinary ethical imperative that is powered in two ways. First, the imperative asks Israel to do for others what has been done for it. You were displaced and were given a place. Now you give a place to the displaced. Second, and more powerfully, you do what God does. God loves the stranger . . . you love the stranger. God gives food and clothing . . . you give food and clothing. You be the social practice whereby God is made visible, available, and effective in the world. You be engaged in God's own work, as you yourself have experienced God's work, creating a safe place of dignity and wholeness for those without rights, claims, or leverage.

Indeed, even Psalm 112 with a lesser passion does not fail to notice that the blessed housed still have their lives marked by generosity that practices right-wising in society:

> They have distributed freely,
>
> they have given to the poor;
>
> their righteousness endures forever (Ps 112:9)

---

10. On the power of this memory, see Ozick, *Metaphor and Memory*, 265–83.

Thus the *tradition of revolutionary housing* and the *tradition of stable housing* both insist, with different voices and different passions and different interests, that the housed must tend to the unhoused, because of history, because of memory, because of identity, because of command. The hot tradition of covenant and the cool tradition of prudence converge.[11] In both traditions, Yahweh is a God who encompasses the life of Israel with a larger passion, a passion that works against one's immediate perceived vested interest for the sake of others.

I cite three texts as a baseline, a beginning point: House as *gift and promise* (Deut 6:10–13), house *as reward for virtue* (Psalm 112), and house as *obligation to the stranger* (Deut 10:12–22). All of these beginning points suggest a triangle: humanity, God, and house. House is given by God; house is definitionally for humanity.

A Loᴣᴣ of Rootage

As you know, Israel's social foundation in the Exodus, covenant and wisdom, did not hold. Israel largely succumbed to a practice of greed which was systemic in character, but which had concrete pay-outs in human misery and human rage. It is clear that the disenfranchised in Israel are not regarded as "the unfortunate," or as the "less fortunate," as though social reality was a great mystery that happens without identifiable agent. Israel demystifies the process whereby poverty and homelessness are generated. The disenfranchised are seen to be victims of a rapacious economic system which had lost its rootage in Exodus (by forgetting), in covenant (by not listening), and in wisdom (by being stupid). The texts I will now cite comment on the systemic act of forgetting, not listening, and being stupid as the way Israel tried to live its life, scuttling its identity founded in Exodus, covenant, and wisdom. In the period of Israel's great public greed, it is clear that homelessness is caused by economic rapaciousness. It is equally clear, because of Yahweh's governance, that such programmatic greed will lead to disaster.

---

11. On the categories of "hot" and "cool," see Brueggemann, "Passion and Perspective."

Greed and Disaster

Two texts voice this prophetic certitude:

> Ah, you who join house to house,
>> who add field to field,
>> until there is room for no one but you,
>> and you are left to live alone
>> in the midst of the land!
> Yahweh of hosts has sworn in my hearing:
>> Surely many houses shall be desolate,
>> large and beautiful houses,
>> without inhabitant.
> For ten acres of vineyard shall yield but one bath,
>> and a homer of seed shall yield a mere ephah. (Isa 5:8–10)

Premnath has shown that this text reflects a process of latifundiza-tion, that is, the process of big owners buying up more and more land, and necessarily displacing little owners and forcing them to life without a place.[12] The poetry is poignant. "Until there is no one but you . . . you are left to live alone," because all the others have been driven out.[13]

Such people-trashing evokes a solemn oath on the part of the Exodus God who has ordered life differently. It is promised by God that the large houses will be abandoned, and the land will become utterly unproductive. The poet anticipates an enormous reversal of the economic process. No clue is given about how this will happen, because this is poetry and not social analysis. Whatever "secondary causes" there may be, we know the name of the primal cause of the destabilization that is sure to come with such neighbor abuse.

The theme of reversal in housing is echoed in Amos 3:13–15:

12. Premnath, "Latifundialization and Isaiah 5:8–10." See also Dearman, *Property Rights in the Eighth-Century Prophets.* Berry, *A Place on Earth,* has written gracefully and positively about the ordering of a community with safe land in which everyone is "placed" with dignity and well-being. Moreover, he has done so without a tinge of the romantic.

13. Perhaps the man in the parable of Luke 12:16–20 is the concrete em-bodiment of this oracle. This man lives for coveting, celebrates alone, and dies in his foolishness.

Hear, and testify against the house of Jacob,
     says the Lord Yahweh, the God of hosts:
On the day I punish Israel for its transgressions,
     I will punish the altars of Bethel,
and the horns of the altar shall be cut off
     and fall to the ground.
I will tear down the winter house as well as the summer house;
     and the houses of ivory shall perish,
and the great houses shall come to an end, says Yahweh.

Again the tone is a solemn oath on God's part. The poem is God's resolve to do the unthinkable against a society that has not thought before it acted. On the other hand, the threat God speaks to an exploitative society is that the apparatus of religious legitimacy will be destroyed. In the horizon of Amos, the shrine at Bethel is the point for the bad neighbor policies of the crown. On the other hand, the houses of the advantaged exploiters will be lost...winter houses, summer houses, houses of ivory, great houses . . . all will end, because some have too many ill-gotten houses. It is telling that in the book of Amos, this poem is immediately followed in 4:1–2 with a harsh indictment of excessive consumerism at the expense of the poor, an excessive consumerism that will end in exile. The critical poetry of the prophets is not so enthralled of present power arrangements that it cannot imagine what comes next. What comes next is derived from the God of the Exodus, covenant, and wisdom who will not finally tolerate "excessive houses" at the expense of "no houses."

God's Preferetial Option for the Homeless

The covenantal-prophetic theological polemic against distorted housing and property systems is rooted in the character of God. God's passion, however, is deeply connected to human hurt and rage. Indeed, it may be that God's "preferential option for the homeless" is evoked and led by the passions of the exploited.[14] For that reason, I

14. That God should follow the urgings of the oppressed who cry out is the premise of the lament/complaint prayers of Israel. See Kim, "'Outcry': Its Context in Biblical Theology"; and Greenberg, *Biblical Prose Prayer*, especially 11–14.

include a text that may sound odd in this context. It is Psalm 109, the most angry of all psalms. In this psalm the speaker is not the voice of God in solemn oath, but the voice of an afflicted human speaker venting full rage to God against a neighbor.

The speaker wishes to have the oppressor terminated and his family made homeless:

> May his days be few;
>> may another seize his position.
> May his children be orphans,
>> and his wife a widow.
> May his children wander about and beg;
>> may they be driven out of the ruins they inhabit.
> May the creditor seize all that he has;
>> may strangers plunder the fruits of his toil.
> May there be no one to do him a kindness,
>> nor anyone to pity his orphaned children.
> May his posterity be cut off;
>> may his name be blotted out in the second generation.
> May the iniquity of his father be remembered before Yahweh,
>> and do not let the sin of his mother be blotted out.
> Let them be before Yahweh continually,
>> and may his memory be cut off from the earth. (vv. 8–15)

That is, we hear a prayer that the oppressor shall be without social place or social identity.

What is most telling in this psalm is the reason for this venomous prayer:

> For he did not remember to show *kindness,*
>> but pursued the poor and needy
>> and the brokenhearted to their death. (v. 16)

The failure of the oppressor is a failure of *hesed,* the failure of neighbor solidarity.[15] Indeed, the poor and needy in the world of this psalm live by a social contract (covenant) in which the resources of

15. On the psalm, see Brueggemann, "Psalm 109: Three Times 'Steadfast Love.'"

the whole community, that is, the resources of the strong, are shared. This speaker, however, has received no such shared resources, because the strong have violated covenant, and therefore the massive curse is uttered. As a result of such a failure of common humanity, the voice of the abused says:

> I am gone like a shadow at evening;
>> I am shaken off like a locust.
> My knees are weak through fasting;
>> my body has become gaunt.
> I am an object of scorn to my accusers;
>> when they see me, they shake their heads (vv. 23–25).

The speaker finally must turn from neighbor to Yahweh in order to find *hesed*:

> But you, O Yahweh my Lord,
>> act on my behalf for your name's sake;
>> because your *steadfast* love is good, deliver me . . .
> Save me according to your *steadfast love* (vv. 21, 26).

It should be clear, however, that this is not a naive supernaturalism, for Yahweh is social practice as well as transcendent possibility. The prayer is a pained decision to turn from a social practice which negates social solidarity, to a social practice legitimated by Yahweh, which is committed to shared well-being. In this social practice there may be a social inversion whereby the ostensibly blessed will be properly cursed and the cursed will be blessed.[16]

Political-Economic Reversal

Thus the sovereign will of Yahweh (Isa 5:8–10; Amos 3:13–15) and the hurt of the marginal (Psalm 109) converge in anticipation of a great political-economic reversal. Biblical poetry does not believe that the *status quo* when excessively brutalizing, can long be sustained. This prophetic analysis of the housed and the homeless

---

16. On the great reversal, see Luke 6:20–23.

anticipates that the first will be last, that the proud will be humbled, that as Hannah sings,

> Those who were full have hired themselves out for bread,
> > but those who were hungry are fat with spoil. (1 Sam 2:5)

And in the psalmic parallel to the Song of Hannah, the poem comes closer to our theme:

> He gives the barren woman a home,
> > making her the joyous mother of children (Ps 113:9)

The clearest expression of this anticipated inversion is in Mic 2:1–5:

> Alas for those who devise wickedness
> > and evil deeds on their beds!
> When the morning dawns, they perform it,
> > because it is in their power.
> They covet fields, and seize them;
> > houses, and take them away;
> They oppress householder and house,
> > people and their inheritance.
> Therefore thus says Yahweh:
> Now, I am devising against this family an evil
> > from which you cannot remove your necks;
> and you shall not walk haughtily,
> > for it will be an evil time.
> On that day they shall take up a taunt song against you,
> > and wail with bitter lamentation, and say,
> "We are utterly ruined;
> > he [Yahweh] alters the inheritance of my people;
> how he removes it from me!
> > Among our captors he parcels out our fields."
> Therefore you will have no one to cast the line by lot
> > in the assembly of Yahweh.

The poem pictures the wicked who scheme in their beds. The poem reflects the peasant suspicion of anyone who stays too long in bed in the morning on the phone to the broker.[17] Before they even get up in the morning, they cut a deal, foreclose a mortgage, preempt a property. They covet fields, they take away houses. They violate the old promise of "houses you did not build." They play monopoly and turn houses into hotels.

Well, says Yahweh, they shall not "advance to Go." They shall not collect $200. They shall go directly into social rejection. As they "devise" in v. 1, so now Yahweh in v. 3 will "devise" against them. The tenth commandment, "Thou shall not covet," is a line drawn in the sand to protect the poor from the strong who have such good brokers and smart lawyers. Coveting, even if it is legal, will finally bring terror of a very public kind. There will come evil, intrusion, and violation of those who mock the tenth commandment.

"On that day," on the day of social pay-out, there will be grief and sad songs and despair. There will be funerals and suicides. "On that day," the monopolizers will notice that Yahweh takes homes away from those who have seized too much. "On that day," an invading army will occupy the fields. The ones who have coveted will not be able to keep what they have taken.

Verse 5 in this poem is odd, but its point is unmistakably clear. There will be an urgent meeting at the county courthouse, that is, in "the assembly of Yahweh." That meeting will be called to reorder the local economy; the purpose of the meeting is to draw new property lines, that is, the redistribution of the land. And when that meeting is held, there will be no one to "cast the line" for you, no one to protect your interests, to advocate, to offer bids, no one to secure the land. When the land is redistributed, they will be left with nothing, displaced, with no place. They will be like the ones they victimized, and now they themselves will be utterly helpless.

This poem reflects village ethics, a small farmer-elder, railing against the urban economy, against the big banks and the cynical insurance companies, against an owned government and bought-off courts whose horizon does not extend past the class that owns it.[18]

17. On such a social analysis in relation to this text, see Wolff, "Micah the Moreshite—The Prophet and His Background," and his citation of the programmatic work of Albrecht Alt in n. 9.

18. Hillers, *Micah*, 33, rejects the particular social analysis of Alt, but on the whole follows his reading of the text.

The peasants are helpless against such great engines of wealth and power. This social analysis offered by Micah, however, is different, because Yahweh is indeed a source of rescue, a line against self-sufficiency, a threat and advocate, a promiser.

It may be that the strong will go on possessing, able to take their usurpacious action against the villagers:

> Their mouths are filled with cursing and deceit and oppression;
>> under their tongues are mischief and iniquity.
> They sit in ambush in the villages;
>> in hiding places they murder the innocent. (Ps 10:7–8)

In the universe of discourse in Psalms 9–10, however, the problem of the house is redefined. A petition is uttered (Ps 10:12–18). Its first line is:

> Rise up, O Yahweh; O God lift up your hand,
>> do not forget the oppressed. (v. 12)

The petition includes the lines:

> The helpless commit themselves to you;
>> you have been the helper of the orphan. (v. 14)

It concludes:

> You will incline your ear
>> to do justice for the orphan and the oppressed,
>> so that thos from earth may strike terror no more. (vv. 17–18)

The psalm provides a way in which Yahweh, the great housing equalizer, can redress the inequity, and override the destructive self-sufficiency of the complacently housed.

These texts from Isa 5:8–10; Amos 3:13–15; Psalm 109; and Mic 2:1–5, where social hurt and heavenly insistence converge, affirm that the power to produces homelessness will not go unchecked. There is an answering, and an inversion that the complacent cannot avoid.

Hope in the Midst of Devastation

As you know, the terrible inversion, anticipated by the prophets, happened in ancient Israel in 587 BCE, when Israel's rapacious socioeconomic policies terminated in deportation for some and devastation for all. The city became a burnt-out crater. In that terrible moment, responsible hope was required. Gone now are the harshest prophetic strictures; silenced is the relentless voice of threat.

I will cite two texts from Trito-Isaiah, which show a community regrouping, to recover a human fabric that rapaciousness and displacement have destroyed.

Concrete Neighbor-Imperatives

On the other hand, the recovering of a viable human infrastructure requires concrete action by those who have not succumbed to selfishness. Instead of manipulative religious practice (Isa 58:1–5), the rebuilding of the infrastructure which makes human life possible entails concrete neighbor-imperatives:

> Is not this the fast that I choose:
>> to unloose the bonds of injustice,
>> to undo the thongs of the yoke,
> to let the oppressed go free,
>> and to break every yoke?
> Is it not to share your bread with the hungry,
>> and bring the homeless poor into your house;
> when you see the naked, to cover them,
>> and not to hide yourself from your own kin? (Isa 58:6–7)

This must in the end be the primal text for our subject. In quick order, in five quick lines, we arrive at Yahweh's central passion, of Israel's central mandate, of humanity's central hope. It is all "hands on." The ones who are characteristically in bonds and yokes and oppressed are of course the poor. The metaphor concerns economics. The ones who are locked in, in poverty cycles, inevitably lack bread, housing, and clothing. This great triad of neighbor love is at the same time the great triad of Yahweh's passion for a reformed community of humanity in obedience. It is this text that lies below the surface of the great judgment scene of Matthew 25, which brings so close together God's own person and the reality of the needy.[19]

When this new fast of neighbor care is undertaken, light and healing come. The world works again and God is again available and powerfully present:

> Then your light shall break forth like the dawn,
>> and your healing shall spring up quickly;
> your vindicator shall go before you,
>> the glory of Yahweh shall be your rear guard.
> Then you shall call, and Yahweh will answer;
>> you shall cry for help, and he will say, "Here I am." (58:8–9)

The end result is the voice of Yahweh assuring, "Here I am." I am here, where bread, and house, and clothing are shared. And where there is no such sharing, there will be no such healing presence.

New Heaven, New Earth, New City

That great imperative is matched seven chapters later, still in Trito-Isaiah, by the most comprehensive promise in the Old Testament, a promise of new heaven, new earth, new city. That new city with a covenantal infrastructure is characterized by the poet in great detail. The one detail that concerns us is in Isa 65:21–22:

> They shall build houses and inhabit them;
>> they shall plant vineyards and eat their fruit.
> They shall not build and another inhabit;
>> they shall not plant and another eat;
> for like the days of a tree shall the days of my people be
>> and my chosen shall long enjoy the work of their hands.

The poem images a stable, equitable community in which threat, danger, greed, rapaciousness, instability, and displacement do not operate. The promise is that houses will be safe for living, not

---

19. The other text which also seems to play in Matthew 25 is Ezek 34:11–16.

attacked, not jeopardized, not foreclosed, that gardens will be safe and not usurped, not invaded, not occupied, not taxed to oblivion. The promise intends to override the danger of a disordered society. In that society, Amos had asserted:

> Therefore because you trample on the poor
>> and take from them levies of grain,
> you have built houses of hewn stone,
>> but you shall not live in them;
> you have planted pleasant vineyards,
>> but you shall not drink their wine. (Amos 5:11)

The terrible jeopardy voiced by Amos is now in Isaiah 65 over-ridden. All is safe, "all is well and all shall be well."[20] This great promise is a word to keep us from succumbing to despair, even about the housing crisis. The command of Isaiah 58 makes clear that housing is indeed our work to do. It is to be done by caring, obedient people. That human work, however, is encompassed about by the promise of God. It is promised that God will create a new infrastructure of adequate, safe housing. It is promised we know not how. It is promised! It is promised that the present engines of homelessness will not prevail, that coveting cannot last, that monopoly and greed will not have a final say.

Thus the two texts from late Isaiah belong together. The *imperative* of chapter 58 counters our self-preoccupation. The *promise* of chapter 65 speaks against our exhausted despair. Our talk is not a complete solution to the housing crisis, as though the imperative could manage without the promise. Our task, however, is ongoing and urgent, while God broods over ultimate possibility. It is clear in both Isaiah 58 and 65, in both imperative and promise, against both selfishness and despair, that housing is a big deal to God. This God does not play monopoly for God's own aggrandizement, but intends for all to have houses, whether because the righteous deserve a house or because houses are freely given to all.

20. The phrase is of course from Julian of Norwich. See Julian of Norwich *Showings*, 225 and passim. The usage of Julian is of course very different. I cite it to suggest the linkage between spiritual well-being and material justice. It is the hope of prophetic faith that *all* will be well.

I conclude this section on a new infrastructure for exiles by reference to 1 Peter and the ground-breaking study of John Elliott.[21] In his book, *A Home for the Homeless*, Elliott has seen that 1 Peter enjoins the Christian community to provide a home (*oikia*) for the homeless (*paroikia*), that is, for exiles and displaced persons. Further, Elliott has shown that the terms for "home and homeless" in the epistle have concrete socioeconomic significance and should not be spiritualized into evaporation.

Elliott thus suggests that the church, according to this epistle, is under mandate to construct a new mediating structure, larger than the family, smaller than the state, a structure for homefulness, for those who had lost place in the homeless-producing Roman Empire. Insofar as the epistle is linked to baptism, as it is according to critical judgment, baptism becomes a gesture of embracing the work of *homefulness* in a world of *homelessness*.

Conclusion

Finally, I come to draw modest conclusions. We have come a very long way since Hos 14:3, "In thee the orphan finds mercy." But not really a long way, for I have argued that the entire life history of this community of faith is a struggle to be a housebuilding, home-making enterprise in a world endlessly productive of homelessness. As I have shaped our primal memory,

> The early season is marked by gift of homes you did not build,
> and by a demand to imitate God's home-making propensity.
> The middle season is dominated by greed, by big ones eating little ones,
> and by the production of homelessness,
> and the dire warnings of what happens to coveters.
> The late season of displacement issues in imperatives
> and promises the concern of a new human,
> covenantal infrastructure.

21. Elliott, *A Home for the Homeless*. On the "household" as a focus of early Christianity, see Meeks, *God the Economist*; and the splendid study of the Gospel of Matthew by Crosby, *House of Disciples*.

What emerges from this study is that the eye of God and the hand of God's people are endlessly upon widows, orphans, and so-journers, those classic victims of displacement.[22] God intends that the displaced shall be commodiously placed in an ordered, secure human community. God has summoned and formed this Israel-Church-new humanity in order to be a protector, an inventor, an alternative, a gadfly, a subverter, a hope, that the dominant modes of exile-production need not prevail in the world.

It is stunning that the vision of the church among exiles in 1 Peter reclaims the identity of the liberated slaves who rushed to Sinai to rethink and repractice a covenantal human infrastructure. The connection between Exodus at the beginning and 1 Peter at the end can be argued sociologically. They both reflect communities capable of thinking and acting differently. But the connection between the early memory and the late resolve can also be seen in concrete textual usage. It is from Exodus, Sinai, and Moses that Peter writes:

> But you are a chosen race, a royal priesthood, a holy na-
> tion, God's own people, in order that you may proclaim
> the mighty acts of him who called you out of darkness
> into his marvelous light. Once you were not a people, but
> now you are God's people; Once you had not received
> mercy, but now you have received mercy. (1 Pet 2:9–10)

The church is invited to see itself set in the world with a priestly role, to proclaim and practice God's mighty acts, to be the *mode of mercy* that orphans receive from God. Preaching is a chance to let the practice of mercy touch the reality of God's displaced orphans.

I conclude wth four questions that may haunt us as we do the awesome work of preaching:

1. Is it true that some lack a home because some have too much house?

---

22. I know of no careful study of the status of "orphan" in these texts. On the widow, see Hiebert, "'Whence Shall Help Come to Me?' The Biblical Widow." It is fair to translate from widow to orphan in terms of social analysis, because the two shared the same jeopardy and vulnerability when the male protector was lost.

2. Is it true that we seek too much house at the expense of our neighbors, because we ourselves are deeply homeless?[23]

3. Is it true that one cannot care deeply about homes for others, until we find our true homefulness?

4. What did he mean when he said this?

> Therefore I tell you, do not worry about your life, what you will eat or what you will drink, or about your body, what you will wear . . . Therefore do not worry, saying, "What shall we eat?" or "What shall we drink?" or "What will we wear?" For it is the Gentiles who strive for all these things; and indeed your heavenly Father knows that you need all these things. (Matt 6:25–32)

We are, as you know, children of the Holy One who already knows we need all these things—as do the others.

---

23. On the social, spiritual dimension of homelessness, see Peter Berger et.al., *The Homeless Mind*.

2

A Myriad of
"Truth and Reconciliation" Commissions

We are, it is confessed among us, saved by grace: delivered by God's good power from the power of evil; rescued by God's generosity from the destructiveness of our own sin. Most of us, schooled in Paul, will readily affirm that that rescue and deliverance are all God's work, not ours:

> We may be surprised, however, to find in Paul's letters virtually no use of certain words we often employ in connection with righting what is wrong. When he speaks to human beings of their wickedness, should he not call on them to *repent!* And should he not say that, after repenting, they can be assured of the peace and rightness that comes with *forgiveness!* Yet, in all of his references to the righting of what has gone wrong, Paul makes no significant reference to repentance and forgiveness.[1]

The gift of new life is fully accomplished by God and so the themes of repentance and forgiveness leave little to be said.

Of course . . . except that the reception of the free gift from God is not easy, and the truth of that grace is not cheap. For that reason, every pastor knows that there are disciplines that belong to

---

1. Martyn, *Theological Issues in the Letters of Paul*, 87.

the reception of God's grace, tasks inescapably entailed in the reality of forgiveness.

Relationship and Reconciliation

For the most part, it is not true, as the Psalmist says,

> Against you, you alone have I sinned,
>> and done what was evil in your sight. (Ps 51:4)

It was not true even for David who recited—according to the superscription—this psalm; he had sinned against God to be sure, but also against Uriah and Bathsheba (2 Sam 12:9). Characteristically our distorted lives violate our relationship both with God and with neighbor. That is why, along with the "first commandment" there is always a "second like unto it" (Mark 12:29–31). As violation of Torah characteristically involves both God and neighbor, so the work of forgiveness relates both to God and neighbor.

I take it that this double fruit of sin and the commensurate double task of receiving forgiveness were in Jesus' purview in his teaching in the Sermon on the Mount:

> So when you are offering your gift at the altar, if you remember that your brother or sister has something against you, leave your gift there before the altar and go; first be reconciled to your brother or sister, and then come and offer your gift. (Matt 5:23–24)

A "gift at the altar" might indeed be a fresh approach to God, an acknowledgment of God's rule, an articulation of gratitude for right or restored relationship with God. One cannot come to such a gift-giving enterprise with God, however, until there is reconciliation with the neighbor who has a grievance.

In the teaching of Jesus the term "reconcile" is left uninflected. We may take it to mean, whether by word or by act, to right a wrong. Such a righting of a wrong clears the way to continue the journey to the altar for gift-giving to God as an act of acknowledgment, an articulation of gratitude, and restoration of that relationship that has been breached. The journey interrupted by neighbor reality, when completed, leaves one in the position to love God and to love neighbor afresh. There is no question in the teaching of Jesus any more than in the theology of Paul that the gift brought to the altar will be accepted. The path to that wondrous enactment of gift, however, is via reconciliation with the neighbor.

Affronting God and Neighbor

It is plausible—I would think probable—that the teaching of Jesus cited above is rooted in the priestly instruction of Lev 6:1–7 (Hebrew 5:20–26). That priestly teaching, amid general and detailed instructions about sacrifices, provides guidance in the priestly horizon to the path to reconciliation. The beginning of the teaching is noteworthy:

> When any of you sin and commit a transgression against Yahweh . . . (v. 2)

Here is a distortion against God that causes a skewed relationship with God. But the text promptly continues:

> . . . by deceiving . . . (vv. 2–3)

The connection between *transgression against God* and *deceiving a neighbor* is by a single *waw consecutive,* the second filling out the substance of the first. Distorted relationship with God is accomplished *by* distorted relationship with neighbor.

The affront against the neighbor . . . that constitutes a trespass against Yahweh . . . is a matter of economics: deposit . . . pledge . . . robbery . . . fraud . . . or something lost and found and lied about. Sins against neighbor that constitute transgression against God are not emotive or private or romantic matters. They concern, first of all, hard-nosed materialism about economic transactions of a systemic kind that block communion with God. The sin is thus double-edged . . . surprise, surprise! . . . God and neighbor! Notice, moreover, that the sin is not twofold. It is one act that affronts both God and neighbor.

Given such an analysis of sin, it will not surprise us that the antidote to such sin is also double-edged and requires the completion of two tasks in turn, the same two tasks identified by Jesus in his teaching on reconciliation.

The first task, according to Lev 6:4–5a, is a full acknowledgment of what has been done against the neighbor, the capacity to
recognize violation of the neighbor for what it is, and a resolve to
overcome that violation:

> When you have sinned and realize your guilt, and would
> restore what you took by robbery or by fraud or the de-
> posit that was committed to you, or the lost thing that
> you found, or anything else about which you have sworn
> falsely. (Lev 6:4–5a)

The agenda of reconciliation matches the detail of the affront given in
vv. 2–3: robbery . . . fraud . . . deposit . . . lost thing. The operational
words are "would restore." The verb "restore" means to return to the
owner what is rightly the property of the owner that has been inap-
propriately taken. Hebrew lacks any subjunctive mood that would
yield "would," but the translation reflects the resolve to do what is still
at the moment contrary to fact. Thus the recognition may evoke an
intention to intervene in order to change the situation. The subjunctive of recognition is voiced in vv. 4–5a. Then comes the imperative
of action:

> You shall repay the principal amount.
> You shall add one-fifth to it.
> You shall pay it to its owner,
>   when you realize your guilt. (v. 5b)

The required action is expressed in three verbs. The first, "re-
pay," is *shalem,* a regular form for retribution that is linked to the
familiar noun *shalom,* thus shalom-making. The second verb "add"
concerns a requirement, perhaps a fine, whereby more is given back
to the neighbor than has been taken from the neighbor. The measure
of twenty percent in addition is a standard one that is required in a
series of practices related to redemption (see Lev 5:16; 27:13, 15, 27,
31; Num 5:7; in Gen 47:24 it is the measure of rent paid to Pharaoh
by sharecroppers.) The twenty percent is clearly a significant amount
of cash for an economic transaction added to the principal, in our
case no doubt to underscore the gravity of the affront, no doubt a
significant amount to dramatize in a face-to-face culture a visible
gesture indicating serious reparation that entails both economic

cost and social face. The payment is a clear, public announcement of a violation, an intentional act to move beyond the violation. In a word, this is *an act of reparation* that constitutes the first step in reconciliation.

It is, however, of immense importance that this pivotal text on overcoming sin does not stop with neighborly reparations. If the sin were only against the neighbor, reparations might suffice. But the affront is, "When you sin and commit a trespass *against Yahweh*." Thus after reparation toward the neighbor, there remains the affront against Yahweh that is constituted through the economic violation of the neighbor. For this, more is required, more that can be affected only through the priest:

> And you shall bring to the priest, as your guilt offering to Yahweh, a ram without blemish from the flock, or its equivalent, for a guilt offering. The priest shall make atonement on your behalf before Yahweh, and you shall be forgiven for any of the things that one may do and incur guilt thereby. (Lev 6:6–7)

The offering to be given is a "ram without blemish" or an equivalent, an animal of immense value in an agricultural economy. Such an animal is the best, the most expensive that can be offered. This particular priestly manual skips over the detail of slaughter and sacrifice, and characteristically offers no interpretation of the meaning of the act concerning how or why the offering of an animal accomplishes reconciliation. The priests seem committed to the proposition that the *act*—without any "theory of atonement"—accomplishes what must be accomplished in the broken relationship within the fractured relationship with Yahweh. Thus the conclusion in v. 7 is that the priest "makes atonement," that is, accomplishes reconciliation. The outcome is forgiveness. The point that strikes me as important is that the priest effects the reconciliation, something the penitent cannot do for himself/herself. I judge that the priest is essential because the transaction is essentially *a sacramental one* that depends upon a credible, sustainable communal world of symbolization in which the guilty party is willing to participate by offering a costly contribution that becomes a vehicle and sign of moving past the affront against Yahweh.

Reparation and Submission

I suggest that we can learn something important by considering an interface between the two texts in Matt 5:23–24 and Lev 6:1–7. The priestly construction of Lev 6:1–7 consists in two actions, *a neighborly reparation* and a *sacramental submission* to the mystery of divine forgiveness. Both acts in turn are expensive, first repayment plus twenty percent to the neighbor and then a flawless ram, a male animal upon which the future of the flock depends. The teaching of Jesus in Matt 5:23–24 does not correlate precisely with the text of Leviticus, even though it is clearly reminiscent of it. In the Matthew text the circumstance, not unlike that of Lev 6:2–3, is one of alienation when "your brother or sister has something against you," that is, the brother or sister has been affronted. The cause of alienation is not as specific here, but the critical remedy is parallel: First be reconciled to your brother or sister. The verb "be reconciled" is not inflected or exposited at all, but one may imagine that the act of reconciliation requires a substantive gesture of some kind, perhaps a verbal sign of apology and/or abasement, or perhaps a more substantive gesture commensurate with the substantive nature of the affront. One may imagine that the requirement constitutes something of a serious act of submission to the wronged brother or sister, more than a generic gesture found adequate in therapeutic society. Of course one must conclude that the act is one of reparation that is indispensable for reconciliation.

With that act completed, one may approach the altar with a gift. To be sure, this teaching of Jesus is not directly about "atonement" nor is the gift identified as a "guilt offering." Only two things are clear. First, the reconciliation remains incomplete without an approach to the altar, suggesting that more is entailed in forgiveness than simply a transaction with the neighbor. And second, an approach to the altar is not empty-handed, but with a gift that signifies a personal, serious engagement in approach to the place of Presence. It takes no stretch of imagination to see that in this teaching, like that of Leviticus, two acts are required in sequence, neighborly reparation and sacramental submission, both requirements entailing giving something of self away in acts of divestment and gestures of vulnerability.

Altar and Text, Sacrament and Word

It is worth noting that neither text offers any theory of atonement or any explanation about how restoration of relationship is accomplished. Nor does the text tell against a theology of unconditional grace, for it is an act of grace that God has provided these means for restoration, the means of *the altar* and its sacramental capacity and, derivatively, the means of *the text* that guides, also a gift of grace. The *altar* and *text*, *sacrament* and *word*, are both gifts of God for the completion of the tasks of the reception of God's forgiveness.

Grace offered by sacramental and textual means must be actively received, in both cases by costly gestures toward God and toward neighbor. By focus upon the two steps in both texts (*reparation and sacramental submission*), it occurs to me that this twofold requirement correlates with the work of the "Truth and Reconciliation Commission" in South Africa. However that title for the commission came about, the phrasing is a mouthful of evangelical theology. The phrase recognizes a two-step process of reconciliation and understands how it is that the two steps are in sequence. The Truth and Reconciliation Commission of course is easily criticized for being inadequate in many ways. It is to be recognized, nonetheless, that its enactment was in an arena of remembered violence and a bottomless deposit of present alienation of a most powerful kind. The task of the commission concerns the revivification of society in the midst of a real life-and-death struggle . . . nothing pretty.

The first step in such reconciliation is *truth*. The truth must be told about a violation of neighbor, and every "violation" perforce participates in *violence*. The truth must be told about violence perpetrated by one neighbor against another. In Leviticus 6, the violence is economic; in Matthew 5, the affront is unnamed, simply "something against you." The violence must be named and owned; gestures of compensation, remorse, and reconciliation for an alternative must be articulated, perhaps verbally, perhaps concretely in monetary terms. The overcoming of alienation is not cheap or easy, but requires truth-telling whereby the offender is placed at the behest of the offended in some concrete way.

Only when *truth* is told, can approach be made to the altar of atonement, that is, to the place of reconciliation. Reconciliation is finally not in the hands of the neighbor. It is in the hands of the priest (explicitly in Leviticus 6, surely implied in the "altar" of Matthew 5), the one charged with nurturing and practicing the most elemental signs of holiness to which the community attests. The priest in both cases, on behalf of the present holy but unseen God, receives the gift, something of value. Of course in such a transaction there are risks of bribery and reciprocity and even Anselm's notion of "satisfaction." The gift must nonetheless be offered as a gesture of submission, divestment, and vulnerability, the ceding over of one's life to the mysterious worship of God's holiness. In sacramental awareness, we do indeed leave the altar differently, for the altar constitutes an arena for the transaction of "trans-substantiation" that is better left unexplained because more happens than can be explained.

Vehicles of Restoration

As I thought about these two texts, the condition of our society, and the pastoral office, it occurred to me that we live in a social context where guilt and therefore forgiveness have been trivialized to be irrelevant, whether it is a matter of rote repetition of "confession and assurance" or whether it is a mumbled whisper of embarrassment.

We live in a society that is deeply alienated; but we also live where the church and its pastors have entrusted to it the awesome, grace-given vehicles of restoration. The recovery of pastoral practices of reconciliation might include the two steps outlined by the priests that are echoed by Jesus:

1. *Truth-telling reparation toward affronted neighbor*, a truth-telling that might be concerned with large, public alienations or it might be so concrete as alienations within families or congregation. The church may indeed be the arena for truth-telling that does not grovel in guilt but that readily undertakes the first step in reconciliation.

2. *Sacramental reconciliation* that requires a priestly enactment of divine reception of costly self-submission and a verdict that the gift is adequate . . . made adequate by the gracious God who receives. On this latter point, I have pondered pastoral authority. I am of course aware of the abusive misfortune of the old priestly

notion of "absolution" that is an affront to evangelical Christians. That old priestly practice smacked of authoritarianism and a hint of two-tiered notion of church, of first-rate priests and second-rate laity. In the place of that practice, however, we have largely forfeited the priestly performative act of reconciliation that, I have no doubt, requires a formal priestly utterance done with gravitas commensurate to our ocean of alienation and appropriate of the new life that is born in, with, and under priestly utterance. A general good feeling or a therapeutic affirmation is no adequate substitute for a priestly performative verdict about the willingness of God to receive our submitted, divested, vulnerable selves.

An Environment of Grace and Gratitude

The dramatic capacity of the church and its pastors in this regard is an astonishing, wondrous counterforce to the world of alienation that is all around us. There is, moreover, no other way to have the vicious cycles broken, and therefore we endlessly repeat the patterns of alienation that inevitably culminate in deathliness.

My son John teaches in a fairly typical college social science department. He has observed over time that in every departmental meeting in his work, all the old hurts and alienations are endlessly reiterated over and over among colleagues. (I myself have seen traces of such faculty transactions in a somewhat different venue.) John, no mean theologian, observed: "The endless reiteration of such pain is because none of the colleagues are believers. Consequently, they have no way to break the cycles of anger." What an insight so pertinent to our society!

Entertain that the church has entrusted to it by God the means of grace—*neighborly reparations* and *sacramental submissiveness*—that can break vicious cycles of alienation and make restoration to life possible. That evangelical reality is of course an embarrassment in a society where *truth* is rarely told and *reconciliation* is most often cheap and surface. The enactment of such an alternative is at the core of our faith, however it is that we speak of "atonement." At the center of such activity is the pastor who has more entrusted in the pastoral office than we usually notice. If we were more self-aware of what belongs to the pastoral office, then we might recognize that what we do in the pastoral office is to conduct and enact myriads of "Truth and Reconciliation Commissions." Such commissions occur randomly here and there; they have their primal locus in the weekly liturgy of forgiveness where all of the grace of our Lord Jesus Christ and where all of the needfulness of God's people is dramatized, and where the fullness of God's grace is made available. In that centered environment of grace and gratitude, *neighborly reparation* and *sacramental submission* make sense as they make sense nowhere else. The enactment of such "Truth and Reconciliation Commissions" may be the most important "social action" that we can undertake!

3

Bragging about the Right Stuff

JEREMIAH 9:23–24; PSALM 87;
1 CORINTHIANS 1:18–31

A ll great cities brag. They gather their energy, produce their images of success and prosperity, and unleash their propaganda in ads, slogans, and campaigns. They do so because they know, intuitively, that stories of success and prosperity draw people, mobilize resources, generate jobs, accumulate wealth, and eventually—raise the standard of living—for some.

Jerusalem's Boast

No great city ever did a better job of bragging than that ancient city of Jerusalem in the Old Testament. Beginning with David and especially with Solomon, Jerusalem gathered its poets and storytellers and liturgists and ad men and sloganeers and made its claim for its urban elite. The bragging took the form of liturgic theology:

> God is our refuge and strength,
>> a very present help in trouble . . .
> God is in the midst of the city;
>> it shall not be moved. (Ps 46:1, 5)

In the Psalm 87 we read the claim that: "Glorious things of thee are spoken, O city of God." The glorious things are spoken of God . . . the one who lives and saves and guards and protects and guarantees. But when they said glorious things of God, they also said glorious things of the city:

This is the city of God;

> this is the place of the temple;

>> this is the seat of the king;

>>> this is the place where are gathered all hopes and fears;

>>>> this is the place of promises . . . all will be well.

Every great city brags, because it knows that self-celebration enhances life and produces a high standard of living—for some. Every great city brags:

Atlanta, a city too busy to hate.

If you are tired of London, you are tired of life.

Chicago, Chicago, what a wonderful town.

Wonderful, wonderful Copenhagen.

Leave your heart in San Francisco.

How will you keep them down on the farm once they have seen Paris?

New York, New York, the city that doesn't sleep . . .

Glorious things of thee are spoken, Zion, city of our God!

Glorious things of thee are spoken, Atlanta, London, Chicago, Copenhagen, San Francisco, Paris, Atlanta, Jerusalem. Glorious things!

No great city ever did a better job of bragging than that ancient city of Jerusalem in the Old Testament. Beginning with David and especially with Solomon, Jerusalem gathered its poets and storytellers and liturgists and ad men and sloganeers and made its claim for its urban elite. The bragging took the form of liturgic theology:

> God is our refuge and strength,
>> a very present help in trouble. (Ps 46:1)

> God is in the midst of the city;
>
> > it shall not be moved. (Ps 46:5)

In the psalm we read, it is claimed that: "Glorious things of thee are spoken, O city of God." (Ps 87:3). The glorious things are spoken of God . . . the one who lives and saves and guards and protects and guarantees. But when they said glorious things of God, they also said glorious things of the city. It is no wonder the wise men in Matthew came looking for the Messiah, the wave of the future, in Jerusalem:

> In the time of King Herod, after Jesus was born in Bethlehem of Judea, wise men from the East came to Jerusalem, asking, "Where is the child who has been born king of the Jews? For we observed his star at its rising, and have come to pay him homage." (Matt 2:1–2)

The wise men had heard all those glorious things. They came, like tribal peasants in South Africa following the light to Johannesburg, sure that they would find there jobs and housing and well-being. It belongs to the great city, or so the great city says in its endless frenzy of self-promotion. All great cities brag about themselves . . . endlessly . . . to the advantage of some.

Jeremiah's Warning

It is likely that Psalm 87 comes early in the Israelite history of Jerusalem, perhaps from the liturgical committees of Solomon in 950 BCE. After that, the city had had a rather mixed history:

- It had had an invasion from Egypt under Shishak;

- It had been besieged by Sennacherib and the Assyrians;

- It had seen a series of minor wars with petty neighbors, Northern Israel and Syria;

- It had a series of bad kings and consequent coups;

- It had prophets arise who summoned the city back to its senses;

- It had a couple of good kings, only a couple: Hezekiah and Josiah.

Then, after four hundred years, about 600 BCE, came Jeremiah, a villager who lived just to the north of the city. He and his family before him had watched the city through its four hundred years of misconduct and bad policy and mixed success. He had listened to the temple liturgy and he no doubt knew Psalm 87, and

Psalm 84: "How lovely are thy dwelling places"

Psalm 46: "God is our refuge and help"

Psalm 48:

> Walk about Zion, go all around it,
>
> > count its towers,
>
> consider well its ramparts;
>
> > go through its citadels,
>
> that you may tell the next generation
>
> > that this is God,
>
> our God forever and ever.
>
> > He will be our guide forever. (Ps 48:12–14)

Jeremiah had noticed the use of the word "forever," a pretentious liturgical term assuring that the way it is, is the way it will be, the grand illusion of the successful and the prosperous about an absolute present tense.

Jeremiah watched, until he could keep silent no longer. And then he commented on urban bragging. He knew that all great cities bragged, but he wished that Jerusalem would not brag about that sorry stuff. He offers a simple triad of bad bragging:

Do not let the wise boast of their *wisdom*.

Do not let the mighty boast of their *might*.

Do not let the wealthy boast of their *wealth*. (Jer 9:23)

But all great cities boast of *wisdom*, *might*, and *wealth*. That triad is what makes a city great. So imagine that ancient city of Jerusalem— or this contemporary city—bragging about its *wisdom*. Jerusalem would do so by reference to Solomon, the king who was said to be learned and wise in every way:

> God gave Solomon very great wisdom, discernment, and
> breadth of understanding as vast as the sand on the sea-
> shore, so that Solomon's wisdom surpassed the wisdom
> of all the people of the east, and all the wisdom of Egypt.
> (1 Kgs 4:29–30)

> He composed three thousand proverbs, and his songs
> numbered a thousand and five. He would speak of trees,
> from the cedar that is in the Lebanon to the hyssop that
> grows in the wall; he would speak of animals, and birds,
> and reptiles, and fish. People came from all the nations
> to hear the wisdom of Solomon; they came from all the
> kings of the earth who had heard of his wisdom. (1 Kgs
> 4:32–34)

Solomon was wise enough to know, and so to control, for he knew
that "knowledge is power." He knew it . . . in downtown Jerusalem!
But we are no different. We are so glad for the research universities, so
glad for corporate efforts at research and development, research that
is never innocent but always in some interest, sometimes business,
sometimes government, most often the military. Because economic
advance does not come with stupidity or foolishness, but through the
awareness of how the world works; and one needs a quota of the wise,
the "stars" of the intellectual world, in order to stay ahead and grow.

So imagine, second, the ancient city of Jerusalem or—this contemporary city—bragging about its *might*. In the city we may boast
of economic power and growth that, alas, invites new roads. Or we
may brag about sports teams, only not just now in Atlanta, because it
takes powerful sports teams—with the ensuing sex and violence—to
be a world-class city. But urban culture is larger than the city. And
eventually might comes to the military. For it is the city that needs
the army to protect its banks and the great concentrations of wealth
and advantage and high standard of living that others want in on. So
Solomon had might to match his wisdom:

> He made three hundred shields of beaten gold; three
> minas of gold went into each shield; and the king put
> them in the House of the Forest of Lebanon. The king
> also made a great ivory throne, and overlaid it with
> the finest gold. The throne had six steps. The top of the

> throne was rounded in the back, and on each side of the
> seat were arm rests and two lions standing beside the
> arm rests . . . For the king had a fleet of ships of Tarshish
> at sea with the fleet of Hiram. Once every three years the
> fleet of the ships of Tarshish used to come bringing gold,
> silver, ivory, apes, and peacocks. (1 Kgs 10:17–19, 22)

And we in our might, so mighty that we "fly over," but get Canadians
and Brits to do the ground war for us, because we are mighty enough
that others will do our dirty work. So imagine, third, that ancient city
of Jerusalem—or this contemporary city—bragging about its *wealth*.
Solomon's wealth came because he controlled the land bridge at the
Fertile Crescent and stood at the center of the global economy:

> Thus King Solomon excelled all the kings of the earth in
> riches and in wisdom. The whole earth sought the pres-
> ence of Solomon to hear his wisdom, which God had put
> into his mind. Every one of them brought a present, ob-
> jects of silver and gold, garments, weaponry, spices, hors-
> es, and mules, so much year by year. Solomon gathered
> together chariots and horses; he had fourteen hundred
> chariots and twelve thousand horses, which he stationed
> in the chariot cities and with the king in Jerusalem. The
> king made silver as common in Jerusalem as stones, and
> he made cedars as numerous as the sycamores of the
> Shephelah. (1 Kgs 10:23–27)

If only it weren't for Charlotte, Atlanta could brag more about the
Southeast, its Fortune 500 world headquarters, and our special share
of the Gross National Product, and better jobs and more growth, and
the "New South," and the matrix of so much of the world economy,
etc., etc., etc.

Three things, said Jeremiah, not to brag on: By now you know
the mantra:

Do not let the wise boast of their *wisdom*.

Do not let the mighty boast of their *might*.

Do not let the wealthy boast of their *wealth*. (Jer 9:23)

They are three items but really all one. One by convergence to have
autonomy and the world on our own terms. Solomon has become a

metaphor in that ancient world for wisdom, might, and wealth. So big, so impressive, so proud, so independent, so safe, so happy. And Jeremiah said:

Do not let the wise boast of their *wisdom*.

Do not let the mighty boast of their *might*.

Do not let the wealthy boast of their *wealth*.

Boast in This

Well, they must have answered Jeremiah in indignation: "Don't you think we should brag, given who we are?" And he answered, apparently without blinking, "Yes, you can brag; but you might not want to brag on wisdom, might, and wealth." And they said, "What else is there to brag on?" And he answered, apparently having his response at the ready:

Let those who boast boast in this,

that they understand and know me, that I am Yahweh;

I act with steadfast love, justice, and righteousness in the earth,

for in these things I delight, says Yahweh. (Jer 9:24)

His is a quick, terse response. Jeremiah gives Jerusalem another triad for bragging. Brag that you know Yahweh, the God of the covenant. This God delights in: *steadfast love, justice, righteousness*. Brag about the things that please the God of Israel:

- Brag about *steadfast love,* about staying power and keeping vows and promises, about long-term fidelity whereby haves and have-nots, rich and poor, and black and white stay with each other in a common destiny because there are no private deals, no gated communities that can be safe, no private schools that can opt out, no protected oases because all are bound to all even as God is bound to Israel.

- Brag about *justice,* about the practice of economic viability in which the great money revenues of the most fabulous wealth in the world is put to use for all the neighbors in terms of health care, adequate housing, childcare, good schools—all readily do-able when the Body Politic comes to know that we are all in it together, that justice is the willingness to submit the economy to the requirements of the neighborhood, in which must some cap their income and their leisure and their self-indulgence in order that all may live well.

- Brag about *righteousness,* a vision of a society in viable, sustainable equilibrium, a harmony of neighbors in which none need to be gouging and threatening others and none need be fearful, because common joy and common hope are rooted in common shalom.

Paul's Theology of the Cross

Well, Jeremiah must have taken their breath away with such a simple, all comprehending contrast: Not brag: *wisdom, might, wealth.* Brag: *steadfast love, justice, righteousness.* The practice of the second triad is of course complicated, but the agenda is clean and simple, and rooted in the reality of God among us.

Jeremiah knows that the city is destined to failure if it continues to brag about the wrong stuff. But Jeremiah knows that even as late as it is, an alternative agenda for bragging is on offer, bragging that is not engaged in illusion and self-deception, but that is rooted in God's own delight.

Boast of the things that belong to God, for these are the very things that make a city work. Paul lives close to Jeremiah because they are on the same wavelength. In his theology of the cross, Paul makes a contrast not unlike that of Jeremiah: God's foolishness in the cross is wiser than *human wisdom*; God's weakness in the cross is stronger than *human strength.*

And then he finishes with Jeremiah:

Consider your call brothers and sisters:

God chose not *the wise,* not *the strong,* not *the wealthy*;

God chose the weak;

God chose the foolish;

God chose what is low and despised, things that are not.

And then finally, "Let the one who boasts, boast in the Lord" (1 Cor 1:26–29).

Perhaps you are like me. Always glimpsing toward *wisdom* in the ways of the world; *might*, in controlling a little piece of the action; *wealth*, not wealthy, but a little more; and then caught short by the teaching of Jesus about *steadfast love, justice, and righteousness*. And so there we are, needing to choose, not wanting to choose, but able to choose and being offered life.

The city, every great city, that ancient one and this contemporary one, wants to brag about its successes and turn out to brag about the very matters that lead to death: wisdom, might, wealth. Imagine that this great church, and dozens like it, exist in the city to witness loud and endlessly to the city that our true ground for bragging is elsewhere: not the fashionable, urban agenda *of wisdom, might, wealth*—but the stuff that delights God: *steadfast love, justice, righteousness*. The gospel to which the church testifies in the city may be put this way: brag! But get it right! Delight in the delights of the God of neighborly fidelity. And then brag . . . endlessly!

4

A Culture of Life and the Politics of Death

If politics is the management of public power, then a *politics of death* is the management of public power in ways that produce fear, hatred, alienation, and brutality. If culture is a web of human signification and interaction, then *a culture of life* is a web of human signification and interaction that produces a community of security, joy, well-being, peace, and freedom.

One dimension of the church's vocation is to foster and sustain a culture of life; it does so by neighborly engagement and by sacramental valuing of the elemental realities of human existence. That practice of church vocation frequently, and certainly now in the United States, must be done (if at all) amid a politics of death that is characterized by an anti-neighborly attitude, an acquisitive economy, and an uncritical commitment to a national security state.

A culture of life is characteristically, and in our setting, a minority report; it is a minority report that bears witness to the intransigent truth of the gospel, that the will of God is for the well-being of all creation.

In what follows I will consider three texts concerning this unequal interface, and then make a few interpretive leaps to our own demanding milieu of ministry.

A Widow in Debt

The Elisha narratives are set down in the midst of the Books of Kings (2 Kings 2-10).[1] They are surrounded by narrative reports on the kings of Israel and Judah presented in highly stylized, mostly predictable royal reports that reflect establishment reality in which little is unsettled or left in doubt. The royal reports have very little generative force. By contrast, the narrative accounts of Elisha teem with unsettling transformative energy. The contrast in narrative style is commensurate with the contrast in substance. The kings, not surprisingly, reflect a commitment to equilibrium, whereas the Elisha narratives bespeak an openness to newness. These latter narratives, the subject of our interest, report on the inscrutable and inexplicable that is evoked and caused by Elisha, the uncredentialed prophet. And while the narratives offer something of the fantastic, they are in fact at the same time grounded in concrete, lived human experience; they characteristically concern life and death matters such as illness and recovery, hunger and food, war and peace, debt and credit. The stories are remembered and told by those who cherish the ways in which this emancipatory agent of life operated within and against the politics of death that was sponsored by the several kings in the narrative. Without any interpretive commentary, it is clear that Elisha embodies and evokes a culture of life that is profoundly subversive of the politics of death sponsored and embodied by the monarchy.

The first narrative I consider is in 2 Kgs 4:1-7, a characteristic tale of prophetic intervention. If we read discerningly, we will see that what Elisha does is to evoke a culture of life amid royal policies of death. The story-line of the narrative is easy enough to trace. It concerns a woman who had bills she could not pay; she is frantic in her appeal to the prophet, because she fears she will lose her children (v. 1). That's the problem. She is in a terrible economic fix! The prophet intervenes, causes a surplus of oil in her house, and instructs her to sell the oil, pay her bills, and live well with her children. It is a simple story of deficiency-to-surplus, from anxiety to well-being. Old Testament scholars label it a "miracle story," and so it is.[2] In that

1. On these narratives, see Brueggemann, *Testimony to Otherwise*.

2. On the patterned regularity of miracle stories, see Culley, *Studies in the Structure of Hebrew Narratives*.

regard it is a fantasy. If, however, we read more carefully, we can see that the narrative is much thicker than that label might suggest.

When we consider the problem with which the narrative begins, we are given two clues to the politics of death out of which the story arises. First, we are told that she is a widow, for she said, "My husband is dead." It is obvious that in a patriarchal society organized around male power, a male-less woman is profoundly vulnerable and is not likely to have resources for life or the means to protect herself and her family. She is exposed and in huge jeopardy. Second, there is the mention of a "creditor," one who loans money, hold mortgages, and exercises immense social leverage. Moreover, we are told that the creditor is about to foreclose on the widow. Before the creditor, the widow is helpless. Indeed "creditor" and "widow" make a perfect pair for the culture of death, wherein the powerful act upon the powerless. The outcome of the leverage of the creditor on the widow is that her vulnerable children may be forced into debt slavery, that is, forced to work, perhaps to perpetuity, in order to satisfy a debt that cannot be otherwise satisfied.[3]

The convergence of *widow, creditor,* and *slave debtor* provides the elemental notice of the politics of death. For the politics of death concerns precisely the absence of a human infrastructure, a complete default on neighborly relationships, and the reduction of neighborly interaction to commodity transactions. The creditor, for all we know, is not mean or rapacious. He is simply committed to the laws of the market whereby debts must be paid, collateral must be held, and defaults must be faced honestly and unflinchingly. Likely he intends the widow no ill, but all parties in the narrative are held to the relentless working out of commodity transactions. One can tell, in this opening scene, that there are no neighborly restraints to the commodity transactions, no capacity for generosity, no sense of shame for exploiting the vulnerable woman, no pathos about the seizure of the children, and no remorse about reducing a family to a marketable commodity. The politics of death is a way of organizing social power

3. There is no doubt that covenantal Israel cared a great deal about debt management. Particular reference should be made to the provision for "the year of release" in Deut 15:1–18. It is clear that such a command is from a different world than the rough and tumble of this narrative account. See Miller, *Deuteronomy;* and Chaney, "Debt Easement in Israelite History and Tradition."

so that leverage is completely "rational" and unrestrained by any sense of the possibility of human solidarity.

The politics of death in turn leads to the elimination of a sense of the public, the loss of any awareness of common membership in and responsibility for society. One can see, in our own time and place, that politics of uncurbed market freedom in the disappearance of the public, in the refusal to finance by taxation any social safety net, a default on health care, an abandonment of public schools, and, in the name of "reform," the reduction of persons to commodities. Writ large, the same perception of reality leads to the shameless pursuit of Islamic oil by way of raw power, without regard for the cultural context of oil or the social fabric of the oil-holding societies. The outcome of such a politics of death is the history of the bodies of dead soldiers, the brutalization and dehumanization of "the enemy," matched by complete indifference to multiple deaths among "the enemy." All of this, I propose, is inchoately in view in our narrative. The widow is a cipher for all those preyed upon by an acquisitive society in the narrow, blessed name of the market.

The prophet is ready and has the capacity to create, amid this woman and her children, a culture of life. Whereas we kill for oil, this culture of life evokes an abundance of oil for the woman, a precious commodity then as now. We are not told how this abundance happens, and the narrative exhibits no curiosity on the point. We do notice that the act of abundance requires the gathering of the entire community; the story goes outside the politics of death and abundance displaces scarcity. The account of the abundance of the widow is a total contrast to the account of the early commodity crisis:

> So she left him and shut the door behind her and her children; they kept bringing vessels to her, and she kept pouring. When the vessels were full, she said to her son, "Bring me another vessel." But he said to her, "There are no more." Then the oil stopped flowing. (2 Kgs 4:5–6)

The home of the widow became a venue in which resources for life are given. The threat of the creditor is lifted and the children are safe. The one with power, in this culture of life, stands in solidarity with the helpless widow who need no longer be vulnerable. The conclusion of the story is the prophetic directive to "pay your debts."

Get yourself out of the politics of death so that the creditors can no longer prey upon the vulnerable widow who need be vulnerable no longer. In the end, *the children are safe!* They are regarded, by the end of the narrative, as social treasures and not as market commodities.

This brief narrative may function as an epitome of the struggle between the politics of death and the culture of life, a struggle that always goes on and that is acute among us now. The narrative, however, is not only a glimpse of the struggle that we cannot disregard. It is also an evangelical declaration of the triumph of the culture of life; this triumph is made possible by the inscrutable working of the spirit of the abundant creator who works alongside a bold human agent and a mobilized human community for the culture of life among those who are not inured in the politics of death.

The Loss of Land

The second narrative account of the politics of death and the culture of life that I cite is from 2 Kgs 8:1-6. In this episode, the mother from the narrative of 2 Kgs 4:8-37 reappears. In the earlier episode, her son had died and her husband was old (v. 15). In chapter 8, the son reappears, the one whom Elisha had raised for the dead (8:5). His reappearance attests to the claim that Elisha is indeed a powerful practitioner of the culture of life. Her husband is no longer mentioned in this episode; it seems fair to assume he has died. If so, she is, of course, a widow without a male advocate, albeit a remarkably resourceful widow.

In the narrative of chapter 8, the woman is urged by Elisha to flee her homeland in the face of an impending seven-year famine. She is for some years a displaced person as she lives "in the land of the Philistines," surely a phrasing used to situate her in a most alien environment, far from home. While she was gone, of course, she lost her land. She was not present to protect her land or defend it legally; in her absence her land was taken from her. Thus the crisis of the loss of all to which she was properly and rightly entitled, lost in the rapacious normality of land transactions. The narrative does not comment on how she lost the land. We might assume the land was taken from her by land speculators, by aggressive lawyers, by sharp dealings that may have been legal but that entertained no memory of her inheritance. On any reading, the loss of her land is a part of the politics of death in which the art of the possible—legally and economically possible—runs roughshod over any human entitlement not supported by social leverage and muscle. However her land loss should be understood, it clearly reflects a politics of death not unlike the situation of the widow we have considered in chapter 4. In both cases, the bereft woman is helpless before the relentlessness of market forces of a ruthless male economy.

Our interest in the narrative, however, is about her reclamation project. When the famine is over, she returns home. She finds her property confiscated or reassigned. She immediately files a petition with the king to reclaim her inheritance. We are not told the name of the king to whom she appeals, but it is one of the sons of the notorious Ahab. As we know from the story of Naboth's vineyard (1 Kings 21), this royal dynasty does indeed practice the politics of death. Among other things, the dynasty managed the death of Naboth on phony charges, declared Elijah an enemy of the state, and handily seized the land of the framed and wrongly executed Naboth. Thus the widow woman must make an appeal for her entitlement to the royal system that practices an economics of death. The prospect of her winning her case before the throne would seem to be remote. We might expect that the king would dismiss her appeal and conclude that her erstwhile inheritance now properly, even legally, belongs to one of his usurpatious cronies. She stands no chance before such a judiciary.

But the story takes a curious turn as sometimes happens in real life. We are surprised to learn that the king, son of the death-dealing Ahab, was having a conversation with Gehazi, Elisha's aide and associate. The servant Gehazi, moreover, knows all about the culture of life that Elisha practices that we file under the rubric of "miracle," for he has had close, hands-on contact with this practitioner of life. The king, curious or perhaps threatened, says to Gehazi, "So tell me about the great things Elisha has done." Give me a summary of the miracles of life he has enacted. This is a strange request out of the mouth of the deathly dynasty, but then, the politics of death is always placed in jeopardy by the culture of life. Gehazi responds and tells the king. He begins with the most remarkable of all of Elisha's prophetic acts of new life. In 2 Kings 4, the son of the woman has died, and Elisha raised her to new life, because he is a bearer of life. Gehazi got no further in his wondrous review before the king's secretary knocked on the door of the oval office. Sorry king, but there is an hysterical woman out here demanding to see you. She enters into the king's presence; of course the king did not know her. But Gehazi did. Gehazi recognized her from chapter 4. Gehazi reports to the king, "Oh my God, it is the woman from chapter 4, the one whose son was raised from the dead." And along with her is the son whom Elisha restored to life. The son is living, concrete, irrefutable evidence of power of the culture for life that surges around Elisha. It is clear that the culture of life touches everything, a woman without oil, a woman with a dead son, and a woman with forfeited property. Elisha's very presence stirs the prospect of newness in contexts where no newness seemed remotely possible.

The king welcomes the woman. He now knows, because he has been told, that the woman and the son concretely represent a new culture of life that he, the king, can take as opportunity or as threat. When the king is satisfied that he has all the data, he issues his royal verdict: "Restore all that was hers, together with all the revenue of the fields from the day that she left the land until now" (2 Kgs 8:6).

What a surprise! What an astonishing royal decree! It is not what we expected from a son of Ahab. We expected something more like Ahab against Naboth: "As soon as Ahab heard that Naboth was dead, Ahab set out to go down to the vineyard of Naboth the Jezreelite, to take possession of it" (1 Kgs 21:16). We anticipate that the king would say to the vulnerable woman: "Tough luck! The land is now organized for the sake of my entourage and your claim has been legally overridden." We call that "the right of eminent domain," whereby the powerful override the powerless, whereby helpless widows characteristically lose their homes in the name of royal progress. It would have been completely in character to draw such a royal conclusion.

Against our expectation, and surely against the expectation of the woman herself, the king acts for a culture of life and against the usual politics of death that prevailed in Samaria. He delivers the royal verdict: "Restore all that was hers, together with all the revenue of the fields from the day that she left the land until now" (2 Kgs 8:6).

The royal decree meets the petition of the vulnerable woman; what she has lost will be restored! Even though she is alone and has no male advocate, she is guaranteed by the king, restoration to the economy in an effective way, a way making life possible for her once again.

We are not told why the king, against the usual politics of death, signed on for a culture of life. But the most plausible explanation within the narrative is that the king is impacted by the "great things" wrought by Elisha and recited by Gehazi.[4] The inventory of prophetic miracles reported to the king made available to the king an alternative vista of political possibility. Options never on the horizon of the dynasty are now available and possible. This narrative is important, for it seems to suggest that the *prophetic alternative* may indeed spill over into *royal policy,* thus moving in a public way to the recovery of the political economy as a venue for viable, human public life.

Jesus and the Culture of Life

Thus far I have cited two narratives of Elisha. The first in 2 Kgs 4:1–8 exhibits the prophet generating new life in a context of death . . . creditors and slavery. The second in 2 Kgs 8:1–8 indicates that the prophetic alternative may set in motion an alternative politics in high places of power. The two narratives together are paradigmatic for our theme of life and death in the public domain. In addition to their paradigmatic importance, the narratives function serendipitously in Christian reading, for they provide a segue to the narratives of Jesus that exhibit the same interface of life and death in the public domain. Indeed, it is possible to see that the narratives of Jesus are much informed by and patterned after the Elisha narratives.[5] For Jesus characteristically enacted a new option for life and regularly evoked the malice and hostility of establishment types who have a stake in maintenance of a politics of death. In the narrative account of Luke, this contestation is nicely summed up in Luke 19:47–48:

4. The royal decree, no doubt inadvertently, is congruent with normative teaching in Israel concerning the property rights of unprotected landholders; see Deut 19:14; Prov 22:28; 23:10.

5. See Brodie, *The Elijah–Elisha Narrative as an Interpretive Synthesis of Genesis–Kings and a Literary Model for the Gospels.*

> Every day he was teaching in the temple. The chief
> priests, the scribes, and the leaders of the people kept
> looking for a way to kill him; but they did not find any-
> thing they could do, for all the people were spellbound
> by what they heard.

The first party of this summary report, "chief priests, the scribes, and
the leaders of the people," taken together, constitutes the power establishment that has a vested interest in the status quo with its careful
entitlements and the commensurate exclusionary practices that go
alongside entitlements. For the common folk, the establishment did
indeed practice a politics of death, denying access to the sources of
life.

Conversely, "the people" represent all those who experience
exclusionary exploitation by the power establishment and who groan
for an alternative that they find palpably available in the ministry of
Jesus. It is no wonder that the latter are "spellbound" by his teaching and by the narrative reports of his actions. They are dazzled and
mesmerized because Jesus operates outside conventional explanations and makes possible what the establishment had declared to
be impossible. And of course, they recognized that his radical alternative was indeed a gift of life that they had never dared hope to
receive. While the theological point of the interface is obvious, the
sociological dimension should not be missed. The power establishment was denied by Jesus its capacity to control by the dangerous
force of alternative public opinion. The report in Luke might suggest
that when vividly under way, the culture of life has such a generative power that resistance by the politics of death is ineffective and
eventually impotent.

The Work of Preaching

It remains only to observe that this deep contradiction is defining for
the church and its ministry, and consequently defining for the work
of preaching. Preaching is situated exactly in this alternative option,
the declaration of that power that arises in a culture of life that the
power of death cannot resist. There is, characteristically, resistance
in the listening congregation to such a declaration, and indeed the

preacher herself often engages in resistance through the practice of timidity. Much of the church is tamed by and invested in the politics of death. But that articulation and practice of a culture for life is nonetheless an enormous yearning among us. Such words of course amount to an utterance of "great things" in the hearing of the king, but that utterance belongs inescapably to the daily missional life of the congregation. The utterance of that alternative may indeed evoke alternative action. It is never easy and always risky to speak and act against the culture of death. But when we do it, we know concretely that a politics of death can never contain the power for life that surges in such utterance and in such practice. Talk about spellbinding!

5

Elisha as the Original Pentecost Guy

TEN THESES

The Elisha narrative in 2 Kings 2–9 + 13 constitutes a quite distinct literary corpus in the Book of Kings.[1] In terms of content and placement, it is a corpus of literature that suggests great intentionality on the part of the traditionists in celebrating this odd character right in the midst of jaded royal power.

1. *Elisha is the original "Pentecost guy" who anticipates the rush of the spirit upon Jesus and who models the conduct of the apostolic community in the Book of Acts.* Indeed, Elisha may be the first "apostle," the one sent. He is infused by the spirit of God who will lead and guide him into courageous transformative acts in a society that had no reason to expect such transformations.

Elisha's narrative introduction as a carrier of the spirit is accomplished in three parts. First, he is presented as a disciple of Elijah in 1 Kgs 19:19–21. At the very outset he has Elijah's mantle thrown over him, a symbol (or totem) of power and authority. He is reluctant to leave his old life with family and work, but Elijah tersely permits him to get his life in order. And then he "follows," enlisting in a dangerous enterprise out beyond all previous connections.

---

1. On this body of texts, see Brueggemann, *Testimony to Otherwise: The Witness of Elijah and Elisha.*

54

Second, in the scene concerning Elijah's "ascent," Elisha is in deep grief over the loss of Elijah and prays "for a double portion of your spirit" (2 Kgs 2:9–12). It is telling that his bid is not for the spirit of God, but for the spirit of Elijah. He is profoundly aware of continuity (apostolic succession?) and presents himself as heir to Elijah's power and authority.

Third, after the "departure" of Elijah, Elisha recovers the mantle of power and authority and dramatically "parts the waters" of the Jordan River (2 Kgs 2:13–14). The reader is invited to relate the Jordan waters to the waters of the exodus, as has already been done in Josh 4:23; it is as though Elisha is prepared to lead a new exodus, this one to depart the hopeless royal enterprise of Israel. He will replicate the work of Moses. His companions are able to discern, from this dramatic act, that "the spirit of Elijah rests on Elisha."

In three quick paragraphs Elisha is identified as the carrier of the transformative spirit of Elijah. He—with this undomesticated power—is on the loose. He is, moreover, on the loose in the regime of Ahab and Jezebel who had compromised Yahwism, who had no appreciation for Torah mandates, and who practiced an oppressive politics and an exploitative economics. The narrative walks us into a situation where the spirit of emancipator transformation is at deep odds with the order of the day.

2. *The emancipatory intent of the Elisha narrative is to witness to the transformative power of God that is loosed in the world through this human agent.* The narrative—not unlike the Synoptic accounts of Jesus—offers an inventory of transformative actions that leave witnesses "amazed," awed by the inescapable awareness that the force of the spirit is back in play against the closed settlements of society:

- Elisha transforms polluted water into "wholesome water" (2 Kgs 2:19–21).

- Elisha rescues a poor widow and her son from rapacious creditors by an act of neighborly abundance (4:1–4).

- Elisha gives a son to the Shunammite woman and then raises him from the dead (4:32–37).

- Elisha transforms poisonous food into edible food (4:38–41).

- Elisha feeds 100 people from a small food supply (4:42–44).

- Elisha heals a Syrian general of leprosy (5:1–27; see Luke 4:27).

- Elisha recovers an axe head from a swamp by causing iron to float (6:1–7).

- Elisha transforms a Syrian military threat into a great feast of peacemaking (6:8–23).

- Elisha eases a famine in Israel by the work of *the wind* (6:24–7:20; note 6:6).

- Elisha causes a widow to receive back her forfeited property (8:1–6).[2]

- Elisha anoints a new Israelite king, thus initiating a dramatic social revolution in Israel (9:1–16).

The list of transformative deeds is breathtaking when it is recited in sum. Remarkably, Israel's narrative exhibits no curiosity about these extraordinary events, nor does it offer any explanation. It is content to tell! The narrative permits the reader to discern, from episode to episode, that something beyond conventional human management is underway in this collection of "miracles."[3]

3. *The deconstructive intention of the Elisha narrative is to expose monarchs in Israel as impotent and irrelevant to the promissory history of God.* The Elisha narratives do not happen in a vacuum, but are situated in a larger body of texts titled "Kings." The presumptive subject of the narrative of "Kings" concerns the kings who rule in Samaria and Jerusalem. The Elisha narrative, moreover, is framed in

---

2. In this narrative text it is the king, and not the prophet, who acts. The narrative reports, however, that the king has been much interested in "the great things" of Elisha, that is, the wonders he has performed. It is reasonable, I suggest, to think that the narrative exhibits the king as instructed and empowered by the wonders of Elisha to enact precisely such a wonder in his own sphere of power, namely, the recovery of the property of the widow that is in the right of the king. If this connection is credible, then the king acts in this way only because of the empowering report of Elisha.

3. It is conventional in critical scholarship to identify these Elisha narratives as "legends," a label that serves to dismiss them because they do not conform to conventional reason. A post-critical reading of them, however, suggests not that they are second rate, but that they open a newness not available to conventional categories. A reflection on such a dismissive use of the label of "legend" lets us observe the way that conventional criticism serves conventional management of social power.

2 Kgs 1:17–18 by a report of the death of Ahaziah (son of Ahab) and the ascent to the throne of Jehoram (another son of Ahab). At the conclusion of the narrative of Elisha, it is framed by a report of the ignoble death of Jezebel (2 Kgs 9:30–37). It is reported that after dinner Jehu, the one dispatched by Elisha to eliminate that dynasty, found nothing left of the rejected queen except "the skull and the feet and the palms of her hands" (v. 36), a residue of failure that signaled, says the narrative, that "This is the word of the Lord." The royal figures in chapters 1 and 9 serve to frame the Elisha narrative, but neither Jehoram nor Jezebel figures significantly in the action that is reported.

Inside the narrative, moreover, kings play only a small role and are regularly reduced to irrelevance.

- In the narrative of Naaman, the Syrian general, the Israelite king responds in dismay and anger to the request for healing, for he is shown to have no healing capacity. Indeed, he himself recognizes as much: "When the king of Israel read the letter, he tore his clothes and said, 'Am I God, to give death or life, that this man sends word to me to cure a man of his leprosy? Just look and see how he is trying to pick a quarrel with me'" (2 Kgs 5:7). The narrative must run on quickly to Elisha.

- In the narrative concerning the war with Syria, the king in Samaria is presented as "perturbed" at the outset, seeking to arrest Elisha (2 Kgs 6:11–12). Absent from the crucial action of the narrative, the king reappears at the end, wanting permission to kill his Syrian adversary (6:21). He is rebuked by the prophet who reminds the king that this is his show, and the king has no role to play.

- In the narrative of famine, the desperate woman pleads with the king to provide food: "Help, my Lord king" (6:26). But the king, yet again, abdicates responsibility and confesses that he has no capacity to make a difference: In 2 Kgs 6:27, "he said, 'No! Let the Lord help you. How can I help you? From the threshing floor or from the wine press?'" As in 5:7–8, so in 6:31 the narrative must promptly refocus on Elisha, the real agent in this account.

- In the narrative of the woman who had forfeited her property, the king is conferring with Elisha's aide and seems to act in response to the woman according to social passions of Elisha (8:4–6). In this case the king does act on his own, but the context suggests that even in this royal act, the horizon of the prophet is operative. The king is peculiarly interested in the "great things" of Elisha that critically break open a closed society.

- In the culminating event of revolution, the prophet has the capacity to anoint new kings and create new political possibilities before which incumbent kings are powerless (9:4–10).

- The cumulative effect of the narrative is to portray kings in Samaria as feeble office-holders who have no power to govern in generative ways. They cannot heal (5:7); they cannot make peace (6:22); they cannot produce food (6:27). They cannot contribute any dimension of well-being to common life, not heath care, not foreign policy, not sustenance. They cannot do anything that kings are supposed to do. The intent of the narrative is to deconstruct and expose them as empty ciphers in the processes of social power that merit neither loyalty nor obedience. The Pentecost guy does not wait on them, but simply disregards them. He is not intimidated by them and offers no allegiance to their empty forms; he has other wonders to enact that make common life possible, wonders over which the kings have no say.

4. *When one considers the wonders wrought by Elisha on the one hand and the impotence of the kings on the other hand, it is clear that the narrative enacts and exhibits a profound tension between office-holders and wind-carriers.* That same tension has been at the heart of Israel's faith since the wind blew back the waters in Egypt at the behest of Moses, an act that exhibited the impotence of Pharaoh, the quintessential office-holder. It is possible to trace that great and durable tension and the great contest between formal power and effective power through Scripture; in the season of Pentecost it is possible to see the effective transformative power that is credited to the force of God. So it is with Amos and Amaziah (Amos 7:10–17), with Isaiah and Ahaz (Isa 7:1–12), with Jeremiah and Zedekiah (Jer 37:17; 38:14–28). And so it is, most dramatically, in the confrontation between Jesus and Pilate. Pilate is exposed as an empty, helpless cipher who administers all the emblems of power but is in fact powerless

(John 18:33—19:16). Jesus, by contrast, has none of the credentials or emblems of power, but effectiveness in transformative activity.

Given that interaction of formal power and effective power, it is no wonder that the apostles, in the Book of Acts, are dangerously on the loose in the empire, turning the world upside down. The Book of Acts is commonly seen as a book that exhibits "the spirit in the church" and as the drama of Easter preaching. What is not noticed most often is that *the Spirit* and *Easter preaching* bring the apostles *before the authorities* who regularly summon the wind-carriers into court. The Book of Acts is a replica of the Elisha narrative. Both attest that the tension in the midst of formal power is a place where all of the Pentecost folk dwell.

5. *"Office-holders" characteristically seek to retard and resist transformative authority and action.* In the Elisha narrative, the king has taken Elisha to be an enemy precisely because Elisha has unloosed transformative energy and authority in his realm: "And he said, 'So may God do to me, and more, if the head of Elisha son of Shaphat stays on his shoulders today'" (2 Kgs 6:31). The king imagines that if he can eliminate the wind-carrier, the wind will go away. In this regard Elisha is viewed in the same way that Father Ahab viewed Elijah before Elisha, as "troubler" (1 Kgs 18:17), and as "enemy" (1 Kgs 21:20). Pentecost characters are always an inconvenience and most often a threat to establishment arrangements. And certainly Elisha in his work of *healing, peace, and food* called into question the power arrangements that privileged some in Samaria over against others.

It was, of course, the same with Jesus. Mark reports, already in chapter 2, that healing and forgiveness are reckoned by the authorities to be "blasphemous" (Mark 2:7), and already in 3:6, a healing provoked lethal opposition: "The Pharisees went out and immediately conspired with the Herodians against him, how to destroy him" (Mark 3:6). The tension between the privileged that guard the settlement and the underprivileged who want access is neatly voiced by Luke: "Every day he was teaching in the temple. The chief priests, the scribes, and the leaders of the people kept looking for a way to kill him; but they did not find anything they could do, for all the people were spellbound by what they heard" (Luke 19:47–48).

The same contest continues in the United States now; the Senate consists mostly in millionaires and billionaires whose work is primarily to channel tax money to preferred lobbyists; only very occasionally can such an establishment body bring itself to care for the common good. *Mutatis mutandis*, what passes for "orthodoxy" in the church as established certitude is a device for maintaining power, whether about who is excommunicated or who is eligible for ordination or any such decision. "Truth" characteristically takes on a strange alliance with power. The office-holders in the Elisha narrative are a powerful embodiment of self-protection and exhibit an unwillingness to run any risks beyond their own protection.

6. *Conversely, wind-carriers characteristically shun office-holding and maintain a distance as "outsider" that gives freedom and energy.* One could not imagine Elisha as a candidate for kingship in Samaria. Nor would one have thought that Jesus might run for governor in Galilee. There are important exceptions to this rule. Thus many of us have regarded Franklin Roosevelt as a wind-carrier for the poor and the powerless; and John XXIII was a wind-carrier who shocked and scared the officeholders in the Curia when he arrived at the Papacy. And Desmond Tutu, after long risky witness, became a bishop. In all of these cases, however, the occupants of the office did not suffer from amnesia. The presidency did not cause Roosevelt to forget the poor. Papal authority did not cause John to turn away from pastoral realism for the sake of pomp. And Tutu as archbishop was not seduced by Anglican punctiliousness away from the critical issues of his society.

These exceptions are important. But they are exceptions. In the Elisha narrative, in any case, the prophet is portrayed as utterly unimpressed by formal authority, unburdened by official responsibility, acting out of a kind of freedom and energy and courage to which "office" could add nothing. Beyond that, his imagination remained uncurbed and unfiltered, so that he could imagine the poor made safe, the dead given life, the hungry given food, the sick healed. He knew in profound ways that the ways things are are not the ways they need to be. Pentecost, in ancient Israel or wherever, concerns the force of newness that is undeterred by present power arrangements. That is why established church traditions, with precious legacies and huge endowments, tend not to specialize in Pentecost.

7. *The labels "office-holder" and "wind-carrier" pertain more to a mindset and an act of imagination than they do to visible, organized*

reality. The social reality of being "in office" or not is important, but I do not think that being "in office" or out of office is crucial. What counts is one's self-perception and one's readiness or lack of readiness to live one's life in a responsive way. Thus in or out of office, one can imagine a safe self that stays close to settled power arrangements and official forms of management and control. Or one can, in or out of office, refuse to be restrained by excessive burden or excessive privilege, and be able to run risks out beyond the treasured contours of any social arrangement.

We do not have access to the way in which Elisha "imagined himself," and perhaps he did not permit himself the luxury of self-reflection, not being a modern person. But we can entertain the prospect that Elisha—or Elijah before him—might have been more "contained" in royal Israel by privilege and deference and entitlement. But one cannot, from the narrative, imagine that he would have been restrained or self-centered in his energy and courage for newness. Thus I suspect that Pentecost is the invitation to re-imagine ourselves—since "imagination" is close to the work of the spirit—not as products of power arrangements, but as heirs of life-giving wind that refuses to be controlled.

8. *The core work of Pentecost is to embrace the wind and to yield the controls of "office."* We may watch Elisha in the early vignettes of his life, "embracing" and "yielding." In 1 Kgs 19:19–21 where he is first on the scene, he holds back from Elijah for the sake of his "mother and father." Interestingly Elijah does not press the point, but gives him room for unfinished business. But Elisha does not hold back from Elijah very long; he moves immediately to an act of outrageous newness; he kills the "means of production" of his family for the sake of "following." And in 2 Kgs 2:12, as he asks for Elijah's spirit, he cries out in some fear and desperation: "Elisha kept watching and crying out, 'Father, father! The chariots of Israel and its horsemen! ' But when he could no longer see him, he grasped his own clothes and tore them in two pieces" (2 Kgs 2:12). One can see in both cases that he is processing his new role, his new vocation, and his new identity. We have no evidence that Elisha ever wanted to "go back." Our own sense of self, nonetheless, will indicate that this Pentecost process of *embracing and yielding* is a demanding one.

The matter pertains to us personally in the ways we are always re-deciding our identity and our vocation. It is possible to imagine the self as an essential "given" and therefore fated from our nurture and environment. Or it is possible to think in terms of an emergent self upon whom the wind continues to blow. The move from *essential self to emergent self is* evoked in: (a) the liturgical process of confession and pardon and invitation to lead "a new and righteous life"; and (b) in psychotherapy in which the assumption is that a new self can be nurtured and chosen and embraced.

As the matter of embracing and yielding pertains to persons, so it may also pertain to corporate bodies. Jim Wallis now is proposing that the church in the United States may faithfully accept its identity not as *institution* but as *movement*.[4] The pair of terms, institution and movement, makes a nice parallel to "king and prophet" in our narrative. The king embodies all of the closure and settlement of institution, and the prophet represents in the narrative all the risks and possibilities of movement. Pentecost is the lively possibility of our becoming wind-carriers when we have spent much of our energy to secure "tenure" in our "office."

9. *A Pentecostal decision about "office holding " and "wind carrying," embracing and yielding, pertains to biblical interpretation as it pertains to every faithful practice in the church.* John O'Banion, in his magisterial review of Western literature, contrasts two types of literature under the rubric of "list" and "narrative."[5] By "list"—under which he includes Plato and Descartes—O'Banion means literature that is comprehensive and organized to bring control. By "narrative" he means indeterminate openness to newness. His categories lead him to speak of the "demise" of narration in a way that is reminiscent of Hans Frei,[6] only O'Banion works in larger scope concerning all Western literature. His categories also remind me of Lévinas's defining categories of "totality" (by which he means an all-comprehensive, totalizing, totalitarian offer) and "infinity" (by which he means openness beyond control).[7]

---

4. Wallis, *The Great Awakening.*
5. O'Banion, *Reorienting Rhetoric.*
6. Frei, *The Eclipse of Biblical Narrative.*
7. Lévinas, *Totality and Infinity.*

The reason I cite O'Banion—along with Frei and Lévinas—is that the categories pertain to how a spirit-powered church might read Scripture. Too much, I believe, we read Scripture according to "historical criticism" that is designed to accommodate the text to our reasonableness. But our interpretation of Scripture that is post-critical and open to the compulsion of the spirit might indeed generate new missional energy. I suggest it is worth a long pondering about how to read Scripture as wind-carriers and not as office-holders.

10. *Preachers are caught, given Pentecost, in a deep bind precisely because preachers—like tenured seminary teachers—are "office-holders."* That is, they are accountable for budgets, programs, and membership lists, and these responsibilities cause one to be cautious, prudent, and restrained. But every preacher knows, as she faces *the text,* about the intrusion of the spirit who summons to say the unsayable and to hope the unhopeable that violate everything that is acceptable in "the office." There is no way out of this dilemma, but there is gain in naming the Catch–22 that is at the center of the Pentecost crisis.

I finish with three ponderings about the Elisha narrative and all the Pentecost guys and gals summoned to be wind-carriers. First, the narrative about the death of Elisha may give us pause (2 Kgs 13:20–21). As the narrative works, Elisha's last public act—the initiation of a political coup—happens in chapter 9; he disappears from the narrative until his death report in chapter 13. There it is reported that by accident a dead man was thrown into the grave of Elisha:

"As soon as the man touched the bones of Elisha, he came to life and stood on his feet" (2 Kgs 13:21). Contact with the dead prophet, we are told, caused new life for the man. The prophet is radioactive, loaded with the gift of life. It might matter that preachers should know—rather than being managers or therapists or moralists—that their very bones, infused by the spirit—are radioactive, recruited for the transmission of life. Preachers might claim more for the wind that powers them!

Second, as I pondered Elisha, I kept being drawn back to the Book of Acts. Preachers at Pentecost are more or less stuck with the Book of Acts and the all-too-familiar story of "tongues of fire." But what if the Book of Acts—set in the empire of Rome—is simply a replay of the ancient narrative of king and prophet, of office-holder and wind-carrier? Pentecost, in such purview, turns out to be not about a great charismatic event (though it is that), but a surge of power for life that leaves us always unsettled and on the move. In a society where "our kind of church" exists, we tilt always to the side of the settled. But if Pentecost follows Easter and the gift of new life, then Pentecost is about public power and public history and public peace and public healing and public food. It means to wrest the public out of the hands of the office-holders.

Third, after Elisha and the Books of Acts, Pentecost is a special time to consider how the people of God position themselves in a society of fear and violence. It should be clear that the office-holders—right and left—have not a clue about how to reorder and renew our common life. Just like the ancient kings, they are bewildered at what they face. What a time for *talk and walk* that knows that the wind is blowing out beyond our preconceived formulations and settlements. Pentecost preaching is not for magic tricks. It is for the slow, steady obedience to what we cannot grasp. This work enacted by the spirit concerns: the communion of saints, the forgiveness of sins, the resurrection of the body, life everlasting.

All of that is well beyond the ken of office-holders!

6

The Stunning Outcome of a
One-Person Search Committee

1 KINGS 19:19–21; 2 KINGS 2:9–15; LUKE 9:59–62

The work of some search committees is long, complicated, and quite public, surrounded by many rumors and much intrigue.[1] Other search committees operate quickly, quietly, and simply, rather like the judges at the Westminster Dog Show—one judge looks and points to the winner, and the dogs did not even know the process was going on. The case of Elijah as a search committee is of the latter type. Elijah's decision is quick and terse, so terse that he does not say anything. He finds Elisha doing field work (with twelve yoke of oxen!), and he throws his mantle over him. The choice is decisive; the deed is done irreversibly, and Elisha knows it: "Let me kiss my father and my mother, and then I will follow you" (1 Kgs 19:20). No discussion, no negotiation, no terms of call.

For these days, I have had search committees on my mind, as had Elijah. Be assured, I am not thinking here of the search for a president that ended happily with Laura Mendenhall. There is no need to talk about that, for it is a done deal and we are all elated. Out of this text, rather, I imagined the great Association of Theological

1. This sermon was preached at Columbia Theological Seminary on April 25, 2001, in connection with the inauguration of President Laura Mendenhall.

Schools Accrediting Agency in the sky consisting in One Person—or Three Persons in one substance, depending on how one counts—conducting a search for just one responsive seminary. I imagined that the search is quick and quiet and simple, so that most do not know the search is underway. Imagine just now, just today, just in our imagination that search committee is eyeing this seminary, anticipating that this might be the one for the coming days of mission. And if the Search Committee in the sky reaches such a conclusion, then it will, of course, accord with what many of us think anyway, that this seminary *is* the one for the coming days of mission.

Responding to the Call

Elisha's response to Elijah's search decision is quick and short and to the point. He says, "I will follow you." I am ready. I just need to do three quick things, and then I follow without reservation.

One: Elisha wraps the mantle tight around his body, the palpable sign of God's summons, to see how it feels and how it fits, to be reassured that there is a workable match between the call and the mantle or alternatively, as we say, to see if for him there is a convergence of "deep gladness and the world's deep need."

Two: Elisha wanted to go home and kiss his mom and dad. Perhaps he wanted their permission. Maybe he wanted them to appreciate and affirm his high calling. Or perhaps he was frightened enough that he did not want to soar off into newness without firm rootage. He did not slough off his parents; he valued them.

It occurs to me that, like Elisha, the seminary picked by the great Accrediting Agency for the new season of mission in the twenty-first century better kiss parents and ancestors. It better touch the past, better treasure the heritage, better remember the best hopes and dreams all the family has entertained before now. And I imagine, as was said about Abraham Heschel when he left his Jewish ghetto in Poland and went off to study in Berlin, that he had a two-way ticket and must have often returned to kiss his mother and father, for what is asked of him now is connected to what is old and treasured.

Three: Elisha took the twelve yoke of oxen with which he was plowing (he was like most Columbia Seminary folk, quite upper middle class). He killed and butchered them and had a great feast. Everyone in the village was so excited about his call that they lavished their endowment on the future. No keeping back ten or eight or six or even two oxen for a rainy season; the feast to mark a time of glad obedience must be extravagant; no parsimony when the search committee acts.

And then says the narrator, he set out to follow Elijah:

> test the call with the mantle;
>> embrace the tradition with a kiss;
>>> lavish the endowment on the future.

A Double Portion of Your Spirit

And then, in the next episode, Elisha watched Elijah ascend. He pleaded with Elijah: Please let me inherit a double portion of your spirit. I take it he means the spirit of God that had infused Elijah. Elisha knew what he needed. He needed the "force of God" for the dangers ahead, the force that would matter decisively—after he had tested the call with the mantle; after he had embraced the tradition with a kiss; after he had lavished the endowment on the future. Elisha needed more than he could control or enact. He needed a gift from God.

He picked up the mantle, now ready. He struck the water of the Jordan, and it parted! He did a new Exodus like Moses, what we used to call "God's mighty deed in history." The community of supporters gathered around him. They were shrewd observers, like an ordination commission, and they said: "The spirit of Elijah rests on Elisha." Search process completed!

He asked for a double portion, and he received it. And he never looked back! He was blown by the wind into places he had never thought to go, to enact things he had never thought to do. Now I know this is just an inaugural festival; it is not a Pentecost. But notice that "following" creates the conditions whereby the "force" is given that moves the nominee into a new range of activity, into a future radically different from his past.

Amidst Scarcity and Death

Then follows the work of the wind through this Elisha. The future is given in Israel through this mantle-wearing, parent-kissing, oxen-butchering, wind-blown disciple. The spirit propels this called one into a concrete *economic situation of poverty and scarcity* (2 Kgs 4:1–7). Elisha meets up with a widow whose life is to be shut down by a creditor. The narrative uses specifically economic terms of "creditor/debtor"; Elisha plunges into the middle of the crisis. He overwhelms the hapless widow with oil, that most precious commodity. All the neighbors bring their pots and pans; the oil keeps running, because it takes a village to receive all the new gifts. In the end, the woman pays all her debts and can live again. The narrator does not ask how this happened, but the answer would have been: a double portion of the spirit!

The spirit pushes the candidate to commit *an overt ecumenical act,* a ministry outside his well-defined Israel (2 Kgs 5:1–19). Naaman, the Syrian general, grudgingly comes to Elisha with leprosy, and he is healed. So Jesus remembers: "There were also many lepers in Israel in the time of the prophet Elisha, and none of them was cleansed except Naaman the Syrian" (Luke 4:27).

The healed general offers to pay for the healing, but Elisha refuses. Then the general apologizes to the prophet, and says, "You know, I am a political general and when I return home, I will be in a media-event in the cathedral, worshipping Rimmon, a God other than the one that has healed me." Elisha, great ecumenist that he is who anticipates later pluralism, says to him, "Shalom, go in peace," that is, "never mind."

The prophet who succeeds Elijah is dispatched by the spirit *into the world of death,* there to enact God's gift of life (2 Kgs 4:32–37). He had given to the Shunammite woman a son, but the son died. The mother of the dead son has complete confidence in Elisha, and so the prophet goes to the dead boy, prays, breathes mouth to mouth with the *ruach,* and the boy lives. The narrative lets us see that this double-portioned carrier is an Easter force for life in a world where the power of death is vibrant and pervasive. In the narrative life will win, carried by the prophet.

The prophet is led by the spirit to an *intimate pastoral crisis where there is a lack of food* (2 Kgs 4:42–44). That lack signifies that God's creation is not fully functioning. There is such a mismatch of need and resources, only twenty loaves of barley, and then abruptly... he feeds them. The bread is passed under his double spirit; we are told that a hundred people ate. They ate and had some left, according to the word of the Lord. This act, so laden with Eucharistic thickness, anticipates the feeding Jesus will do.

These acts constitute an amazing catalogue of transformative miracles:

- an economic intervention that redresses the life of creditors and debtors;

- an overt ecumenical act that values those unlike "us";

- an Easter foray into the sphere of death to bring life;

- a pastoral of feeding, bespeaking the generosity of the Creator.

No doubt all of these stories are designed to celebrate and enhance this remembered figure of power who had *a cloak, a kiss, a festival*, and worked in awesome ways to make things new. No doubt all the stories, theologically self-conscious, witness to God's governance in the large and small places of the world where it was thought they were autonomous. In truth, these stories are not simply about God's governance, or simply about the oddness of the prophet, but about the *strange, unfamiliar convergence of human agency and divine sovereignty allied for a newness that the world had not yet imagined*. The stunning outcome of this search process was the release of power for life in a world weary with the gap between creditors and debtors, exhausted with faith turned in on itself exclusively, despairing in the face of the power of death to which there seemed no antidote, fed up with so many little children to feed and not enough bread. Here we are treated not to explanations, but only to a terse summons, a rush of energy, God's power for life given concrete, fleshly form. We are brought up short before the power for life that is so unspeakable that when Elisha dies several chapters later they threw another dead body into his grave with his body, and that one came alive when it touched the still bones of Elisha (2 Kgs 13:20–23). This double-portioned man continues, it is said, to be a force for life even in his own death.

Of course this is all legend. It is remote from us. It is personal and not institutional, spun by the spirit and not at all decent and in order. It has, surely, nothing to do with us. Except we never know with a *cloak* and a *kiss* and *oxen butchered*, and the force sent anew.

Do Not Kiʃʃ a Corpʃe

You will notice I have not yet come to the Gospel reading. As usual, Jesus is more radical than the antecedents in Israel. Elijah let his designee go kiss his mother and father. Jesus said, "Forget about them." Jesus seems to call to a more radical break—no time to go home first. But the cases are not quite parallel. Evidently Elisha's mother and father are alive and well, functioning and supportive of this new place where deep gladness and the deep need of the world converge. In the second case, the father is already dead. In that case, the demand is sharper: Do not go back to death. Do not kiss a corpse.

It occurs to me that when the great Accrediting Agency in the sky points, one task for the designee is to sort out vibrant, pertinent antecedents and failed antecedents that will give no life. Jesus' word is: do not spend energy on failed antecedents, but unload them to travel light in obedience.

Perhaps:

- leave off old memories that are small and suffocating;

- leave off old speeches that seem to need one more utterance in one more meeting;

- leave off pet projects whereby an incidental has become definitional;

- leave off old hurts and affronts that are revisited too often to permit healing;

- leave off the shrillness that always needs to make one more "statement";

- leave off old fears and hates and angers that block the wind, old modes of doctrine (liberal or conservative) that are only cultural accidents, and old moralities (liberal or conservative) that are, in fact, disguised fear and vested interest.

The one he addressed was ready, but said: "I will follow you Lord; but let me first say farewell to those at my home." Jesus, however, is an impatient search committee: "None who puts a hand to the plow and looks back is fit for the kingdom of God" (Luke 9:62). So imagine a Search Committee dreaming of the coming governance:

—we with a cloak of emancipated responsibility;

—we with vibrant mothers and fathers to embrace and failed mothers and fathers to relinquish.

—we with twelve oxen or more, but not finally dependent on market fluctuations.

—propelled into economic situations of creditors and debtors;

—pushed into ecumenical contexts, healing among those who are long time outsiders and alien to us;

—dispatched into a world where death is strong, in order to enact gestures of new life;

—led into intimate places of need to feed and house and cloth, with as many as twelve baskets left over.

Seminaries like ours are mostly equipped for the steadiness of twentieth-century denominational patterns. And now come the twenty-first century and the purposes of God in, with, and under and beyond all the structures, categories, and procedures so comfortable and familiar to us.

The Search Committee, so says the text, is able to find a candidate ready to be propelled, pushed, dispatched, led, summoned to the places where "deep gladness and deep need" converge. It is hard to measure the gift of the spirit about to be given among us. But it is, we surmise, doubled in joy and with names written in heaven. Doubled is a lot, more than enough!

7

The Non-Negotiable Price of Sanity

Jesus, of course, was not born in a vacuum, nor did he live in a
vacuum. Clearly his life is bounded by the ambitious, absolutist
claims of "Caesar," a metaphor of the extreme pretensions of human
power and the long reach of empire. Thus at his birth,

> In those days a decree went out from Caesar Augustus
> . . . (Luke 2:1)[1]

At his death, the testimony against him went like this:

> If you release this man, you are no friend of Caesar.
> Everyone who claims to be a king sets himself against
> Caesar . . . We have no king but Caesar. (John 19:12, 15)

Eventually Jesus, in his rule, must come to terms with Caesar
and his power. Or rather, Caesar and his power must come to terms
with Jesus and his rule.

My difficult assignment in what follows is a reflection not
on *Jesus and Caesar*, but on what a pastor in the U.S. Church may
say about the political-economic-military hegemony of the U.S. as
the last, now unbridled superpower. The question is an odd one in
Advent, because we do not usually pose such great public issues at
this season in the Church. The topic has one other oddity for me,
namely, that as an Old Testament teacher, I must transpose the theme

1. The NRSV prefers to translate "Emperor" rather than "Caesar," but the
point is the same.

into Old Testament categories. I do so by suggesting that in the Old Testament, it is Nebuchadnezzar the Babylonian who is a cipher for absolute human pretensions to power and authority. The reader will only need to be agile enough to move back and forth among *Nebuchadnezzar, Caesar,* and *U.S. hegemony* in order to see that evangelical proclamation of the coming Christ child is indeed vis-à-vis big power questions. The big power questions are available because the birth of Christ is always just as "a decree went out from Caesar Augustus." I cite three Nebuchadnezzar texts that readily transpose into our own preaching possibility.

Provisional Alignment

The Bible can entertain the thought that *God will align God's self with a superpower (Nebuchadnezzar, Caesar) on a provisional basis, in order to accomplish a particular task.* The Bible inevitably struggles with the claim that *divine purpose* and *human agency* may be directly connected. It struggles, moreover, with how to speak about that connection. In prophetic discourse, the performance of the connection is in simple, direct, "supernatural" talk, though sometimes the rhetoric is more cagey, as when it is said that God "stirs up" human agents. Such a verb makes a claim, but without any exact "cause-effect" explanatory substance.

In the particular case I cited of divine purpose through human agency, Jeremiah can speak twice of Nebuchadnezzar as *chosen servant, instrument,* and *vehicle* of divine purpose:

> I am going to send for all the tribes of the north, says Yahweh, even for King Nebuchadrezzar of Babylon, *my servant,* and I will bring them against this land and its inhabitants, and against all these nations around; I will utterly destroy them, and make them an object of horror and of hissing, and an everlasting disgrace. (Jer 25:9)

> Now I have given all these lands into the hand of King Nebuchadnezzar of Babylon, *my servant,* and I have given him even the wild animals of the field to serve him. (Jer 27:6)

In this particular case, the divine purpose that is to be enacted is the destruction of Jerusalem, a recalcitrant city that is the target of divine wrath. In this discourse, the "Caesar" of Babylon is dispatched to do the deed (see 2 Kgs 24:10–17; 25:8–21). Now of course, such an incursion by the Babylonians can be completely understood in terms of *Realpolitik* without reference to divine purpose. But that would miss the point of it all, for in prophetic discourse it is divine purpose rather than human agency that is the key issue.

The two verses I have cited from Jeremiah voice a remarkable, even treasonable utterance in ancient Israel, namely, that Yahweh could recruit a foreign power to move destructively against God's own people. Thus the problematic of this provisional alliance between Yahweh and Babylon is in at least two dimensions, first that Yahweh was able to recruit a foreign power, and second, that the purpose is judgment of God's own people.

By the same token, one could imagine prophetic discourse to make a contemporary claim that the God who governs public life has aligned God's own self with the last superpower (the United States), in order to accomplish a particular task, namely, the "regime change" in Iraq. Indeed, the feverish patriotic rhetoric of war comes close to that affirmation. That parallel to ancient prophetic discourse, however, misses an acute point; in Jeremiah, it is a dispatch of an enemy force *against us,* whereas in our preferred rhetoric it is a dispatch *of us* against others.

In order to appropriate the radical prophetic rhetoric of "against us," one might, in parallel to Jeremiah, rather say that the God of history "stirred up" Osama Bin Laden as a provisional tool against the recalcitrant United States. Of course I know of no prophetic figure who wants to say that, and I know of no church where it might be said. The analogue is worth notice in order to recognize the extreme character of prophetic discourse that permits Yahweh to enter into odd alliances, the sort of connection we ourselves would find improbable and scandalous. The recruitment of odd agents "against us" is simply what Isaiah means by God's "alien work":

> For Yahweh will rise up as on Mount Perazim,
>   he will rage as in the valley of Gibeon;
>   to do his deed—*strange is his deed*!
>   and to work his work—*alien is his work*! (Isa 28:21)

An Unsustainable Hegemony

The Bible can entertain the thought that *God's alliance with a super-power is at best provisional and can be sustained only as long as the superpower conforms to the will and purpose of God.* In the rhetoric of Jeremiah, there is no doubt that God is allied with Nebuchadnezzar. Indeed, the entire book of Jeremiah is permeated with pro-Babylonian sentiments, with the conviction that Yahweh wills a Babylonian onslaught against Jerusalem in the same that easy religious rhetoric can now claim that God wills the U.S. devastation of Baghdad. And no doubt the ideologues around Nebuchadnezzar imagined that divine destiny assured Babylonian preeminence for all imaginable time to come, indeed in perpetuity.

But of course it did not happen that way and it does not happen that way; inescapably singular superpower hegemony turns out to be an unsustainable fifteen minutes of fame as every superpower learns late.[2] In the case of Babylon, Nebuchadnezzar died in 562 BCE and within a dozen years it was all over for Babylon. It was all over, because Persia (Iran) from the East became the new superpower to last until the rise of Alexander the Great. But if the superpower that is "my servant" promptly goes into demise, then prophetic rhetoric must speak in a new mode.

That new mode that takes into account the demise of "my servant, Babylon" makes clear that the alignment of YHWH with the superpower is provisional. The prophetic rhetoric of demise takes two forms. One is the claim that YHWH has entered into a new alliance, this time with Cyrus the Persian who now, by divine instigation, will displace Babylon. In this usage, the verb "stir up" is paramount:

> For I am going to stir up and bring against Babylon a company of great nations from the land of the north; and they shall array themselves against her; from there she shall be taken. Their arrows are like the arrows of a skilled warrior who does not return empty-handed. (Jer 50:9)

2. See the notorious claims for empire in Fukiyama, *The End of History and the Last Man.*

> Thus says the Lord:
> I am going to stir up a destructive wind against Babylon
>   and against the inhabitants of Leb-qamai. (Jer 51:1)

> Who has roused a victor from the east,
>   summoned him to his service?
> He delivers up nations to him,
>   and tramples kings under foot;
> he makes them like dust with his sword
>   like driven stubble with his bow. (Isa 41:2)

> I stirred up one from the north, and he has come,
>   from the rising of the sun he was summoned by name.
> He shall trample on rulers as on mortar,
>   as the potter treads clay. (Isa 41:25)

As Yahweh had "stirred up" Nebuchadnezzar in the first instant, so now a second "stirring up" of Cyrus causes new political arrangements throughout the known world.

It is, however, the second mode of rhetoric that here concerns us. In Isaiah 47, in the next generation after Jeremiah, the prophetic poet anticipates the demise of Babylon at the hands of Cyrus . . . at the behest of Yahweh. In this poetry, it is *unbridled arrogance* that imagines *imperial autonomy* that is the cause of the failure of Babylon. The glorious empire—the last superpower—is deconstructed in poetic imagination:

> Come down and sit in the dust,
>   virgin daughter Babylon!
> Sit on the ground without a throne,
>   daughter Chaldea!
> For you shall no more be called
>   tender and delicate.
> Take the millstones and grind meal,
>   remove your veil,
> strip off your robe, uncover your legs,
>   pass through the rivers.

> Your nakedness shall be uncovered,
>> and your shame shall be seen. (Isa 47:1–3a)

The poet places in the mouth of Babylon repeated statements of imagined autonomy that needs give account to no holy ultimacy:

> You said, "I shall be mistress forever,"
>> so that you did not lay these things to heart
>> or remember their end. (Isa 47:7)

> Now therefore hear this, you lover of pleasures,
>> who sit securely,
> who say in your heart,
>> "I am, and there is no one besides me;
> I shall not sit as a widow
>> or know the loss of children"—
> both these things shall come upon you
>> in a moment, in one day:
> the loss of children and widowhood
>> shall come upon you in full measure,
> in spite of your many sorceries
>> and the great power of your enchantments. (Isa 47:8–9)

> No one sees me . . .
>> I am, and there is no one besides me. (Isa 47:10)

Perhaps such imagined autonomy is inescapable in a superpower that goes from strength to strength until there is no more challenge or competition. It is clear in that ancient world that Babylonian power was unchecked; Nebuchadnezzar could do with impunity whatever he wanted.

But of course, it is the vocation of prophetic imagination to assert that because of holy governance such autonomy is a self-destructive illusion. The alliance Yahweh has made with Nebuchadnezzar is a real one that brings honor and victory to Babylon. But the alliance is in order to accomplish divine purpose; when Babylon moves away form that divine purpose, hegemony will fail abruptly. So affirms prophetic faith!

In Isa 47:6, the poet offers a succinct summary of prophetic imagination concerning ambitious world power:

a. Yahweh is angry with Yahweh's own chosen people. That of course is the primary burden of much prophetic rhetoric; Israel has violated covenant with Yahweh and must be punished.

b. While divine wrath is supernatural in its magnitude, the punishment that is to happen is "natural." It takes place through historical modes. Yahweh gives Israel "into the hand" (power) of the superpower. The Babylonian onslaught of Jerusalem is at divine behest! What can be seen is simply Babylonian expansionism. What is uttered by the prophets is the divine instigation of that expansionist policy.

c. But then: You showed no mercy! Now the poet arrives at the culminating message. Nebuchadnezzar was given a free hand against Babylon and enacted that free hand with severity and cruelty. In doing so, Nebuchadnezzar misunderstood his mandate and imagined that he was completely free with his "free hand," to do what he wanted with Jerusalem.

But "no," says the poet. No, a superpower is not given such freedom. No, a superpower is not autonomous in the practice of power. No, the world is not open for any barbarism we may choose. It turns out that Nebuchadnezzar was expected, by the very God who had dispatched him, to *show mercy* upon Jerusalem, the very city he was mandated to punish.

Of course nothing was said earlier to Babylon about divine mercy. Of course military adventurism cannot be "tainted" by mercy. Of course no imperial power thinks or calculates in terms of mercy. Of course! Except—so says the prophet—mercy is the intransigent divine curb on all imperial autonomy, a curb that is intrinsic to the processes of practical politics, intrinsic because it is the ultimate will of the creator God.

I would imagine Nebuchadnezzar replied to this indictment defiantly and defensively, "You never said anything about mercy." I would imagine, moreover, the Holy One saying back to the king, "You should have known!" You should have known because of Sinai; you should have known because of the large covenant with Noah; you should have known because you have seen that the flesh of babies is not amenable to bayonets, because the vulnerability of women is not available for military barbarism, and because you yourself, for all of your macho force, shrink from pain that comes to your body. You should have known because God is God, the God whose wont it is always to show mercy.[3] And because you did not know what you should have known,

> evil shall come upon you,
>> which you cannot charm away;
> disaster shall fall upon you,
>> which you will not be able to ward off;
> and ruin shall come on you suddenly,
>> of which you know nothing. (Isa 47:11)

By the same token, we may entertain the conviction that God has "dispatched" the United States to do a divine deed. Perhaps. But even so, the overriding reality of such a mandate is mercy; and when mercy is not shown, a superpower (Caesar) that takes itself with ultimate seriousness and freedom will—soon or late—collide with the divine purpose that is mercy. Any superpower inured in *arrogance* that bespeaks *brutality* is not sustainable!

The Hidden World of Divine Mercy

The Bible can entertain the thought that *superpowers that imagine arrogant autonomy eventually self-destruct in insanity and recover sanity only by submissive doxology.* I cite the late reflective narrative of Daniel 4 that continues to ponder Nebuchadnezzar who has become a metaphor for would-be absolute worldly power.

This narrative features a confrontation between Nebuchadnezzar, quintessential absolute world power, and Daniel, the wise, endangered Jew. It takes little imagination to transpose that encounter into one between Caesar and Jesus. It takes a bit more imagination to transpose that meeting into an exchange between U.S. hegemonic power and the Christian preacher. No doubt the narrative, in all of its particularity, is a model of *truth speaking to power.* And if one were

---

3. I intend this to be an allusion to the familiar cadence of the *Book of Common Prayer*, though the precise collect is lost to me at the moment.

to be caught in such a conversation, we may ask what should truth say to power!

Here Daniel interprets the dream of Nebuchadnezzar. The dream may be only a narrative device for what follows. But it may also be a recognition that absolute power is inescapably haunted by misgivings and precariousness, for every absolute power is inherently edgy in its awareness of fragility. Daniel's interpretation gives force and specificity to the misgivings hosted by arrogant power. The reason for the misgiving, says he, is that "the Most High God has sovereignty over the kingdom of mortals, and gives it to whom he will" (Dan 4:25b).

The deployment of sovereignty is at the behest of the Most High. It is the Most High God who gives it and who can take it back. Which means, of course, that imagined ultimacy is an illusion; worldly power is held only at the will of Yahweh. Nebuchadnezzar's power is at best penultimate, subject to revision and to termination.

The punishment for imagined autonomy is the deconstruction of power and glory into shame, failure, and humiliation:

> You shall be driven away from human society, and your dwelling shall be with the wild animals. You shall be made to eat grass like oxen, you shall be bathed with the dew of heaven, and seven times shall pass over you. (Dan 4:25a)

And sure enough, it happened as the dream anticipated. No one would have thought that this absolute power would be promptly reduced to grotesqueness, as a voice beyond his control declared:

> While the words were still in the king's mouth, a voice came from heaven: "O King Nebuchadnezzar, to you it is declared: The kingdom has departed from you! You shall be driven away from human society, and your dwelling shall be with the animals of the field. You shall be made to eat grass like oxen, and seven times shall pass over you, until you have learned that the Most High has sovereignty over the kingdom of mortals and gives it to whom he will." (Dan 4:31–32)

The voice is promptly matched by narrative reality:

> Immediately the sentence was fulfilled against Nebu-
> chadnezzar. He was driven away from human society, ate
> grass like oxen, and his body was bathed with the dew of
> heaven, until his hair grew as long as eagles' feathers and
> his nails became like birds' claws. (Dan 4:33)

Now of course, this is a fantasy narrative not to be read liter-
ally. It is not an analysis of *Realpolitik*. It is rather a brooding after
the inescapable reality that worldly power lives in the hidden world
of Holy Governance. Nebuchadnezzar did not know that when he
had sent his armies against Jerusalem. And Caesar did not know that
when he issued a decree that "all the world should be registered." And
surely in the contemporary onslaught in Iraq, the U.S. government
had given little thought that its power lives in the hidden world of
divine mercy. The outcome, so says the narrative, is reduction to bes-
tiality and grossness, barbarism, cruelty, and the loss of humanness.
The narrative does not say insanity, but the depiction is of one who
has gone crazy in self-regard.

And then in 4:34a, the narrative turns: "When that period was
over, I, Nebuchadnezzar, lifted my eyes to heaven, and my reason
returned to me." His reason returned! Which means that his reason
had been lost! It had been lost in arrogance that produced brutality.
The good news for Nebuchadnezzar—and for everyone made insane
by power—is that the story turns. It is possible to get over such cra-
ziness! It is possible to return to the proper limits of penultimacy
in which human power is held in acknowledgement of the curbing
power of divine mercy. It is possible to repent of arrogance, though
perhaps only through a season of humiliation.

Now Nebuchadnezzar sings to the Most High, the one who
has sovereignty over the kingdom of mortals and who gives it to
whom he will. Nebuchadnezzar sings a doxology, which means that
he engages in an act of ceding ultimacy from himself to the God of
all mercy. Doxology is indeed a political act of submission and sur-
render to the one who properly receives our attestation of ultimacy.
Nebuchadnezzar sings:

> I blessed the Most High,
>   and praised and honored the one who lives forever.

> For his sovereignty is an everlasting sovereignty,
>> and his kingdom endures from generation to generation.
> All the inhabitants of the earth are accounted as nothing,
>> and he does what he wills with the host of heaven
>> and the inhabitants of the earth.
> There is no one who can stay his hand
>> or say to him, "What are you doing?" (Dan 4:34b–35)

The outcome is that, I was re-established over my kingdom, and still more greatness was added to me (Dan 4:36). The great usurper has come to his senses, and in the end extols the king of heaven,

> For all his works are truth,
>> and his ways are justice;
> and he is able to bring low
>> those who walk in pride. (Dan 4:37)

Now rule is marked by trust and justice, exact alternatives to Nebuchadnezzar's erstwhile arrogant practice of deception and exploitation. This is not only theological submission; it is also a reversal of policy. For the one who has power is brought low, low enough to see clearly his proper destiny and vocation in a world governed beyond him.

Mutatis mutandis, it is not difficult to see that U.S. imperialism has now gone insane, drunk with self-congratulatory power, intoxicated with self-regard, out of touch with Holy Reality. The news is that this need not be the fate of this superpower, for reason might return, reason that is the capacity to "come down where you ought to be." That of course can only happen if there are witnesses to God who has sovereignty and gives it to whom he will. The narrative makes it possible to see the distance, slippage, and freedom between divine purpose and human agency, a connection that is always provisional, that depends upon conformity to the merciful purpose of God, and that requires submissive doxology matched by policy.

To Haunt, Astonish, and Transform

Now of course I have strayed from the assignment given by my editor, because I had to transpose the theme into the Old Testament and of course I have departed somewhat from a sustained attentiveness to "Caesar" in the career of Jesus. Nonetheless, I believe the issue of Nebuchadnezzar, Caesar, and U.S. hegemony are all of a piece, all seduced to imagined autonomy.

I am aware that in most of our churches even to raise these issues is extremely hazardous. But there is almost no one else except pastors to raise these urgent matters. They do not need to be raised directly or in inflammatory ways. They can be surfaced around good Calvinist themes of the *hiddenness of divine sovereignty,* of *the graciousness of God over the public process,* and *the deathly lure of idolatry.* It is not necessary that the pastor should startle or offend the congregation. It is enough, in my judgment, that the congregation should be haunted in dis-ease about aggressive American imperialism and its seductive power. The ground is ripe among us for such haunting, given the awareness among us that is pervasive because of the Iraqi prison crisis. But how shall the Church be haunted without texts? And how shall the Church have texts that haunt unless the preacher offers them?

It is more than a little ironic that when Nebuchadnezzar asks Daniel for advice on redress, Daniel answers in a way that is characteristically Jewish:

> Therefore, O king, may my counsel be acceptable to you: atone for your sins with righteousness, and your iniquities with *mercy to the oppressed,* so that your prosperity may be prolonged. (Dan 4:27)

It sounds like Daniel had been reading Deutero-Isaiah. But then, that is what poetic, imaginative pastoral voices continue to do. They continue to read texts that haunt and astonish and transform. And when there are enough such texts available, we may from time to time recover our sanity!

8

The Family as World-Maker

The family is, of course, under assault. The structures of social life we have taken for granted are in jeopardy. The issues are expansive and the crisis is more comprehensive than simply the family. A host of anxieties get transferred to the family that properly belong elsewhere. Nonetheless, the family is clearly in crisis as a social structure among us. People rightly ask if biblical faith has resources out of which to make response to this crisis.

The Bible, as nearly as I can determine, contains no single prescription that can be articulated concerning the family. Perhaps if it did, it would not be a single prescription that would be very congenial to the nuclear, capitalist family as is often assumed. In any case, I focus here on *one function of the family*, which I suggest lies at the heart of our social crisis. I propose that counsel directly out of the Bible for families in crisis consists not in ethical advice (not even advice about sexuality), but in an invitation to *practice a peculiar vocation* that is indispensable for the family and for all healthy social interaction.

That practice of a peculiar vocation can be expressed in several ways. Popularly it has to do with storytelling, with building a "narrative world."[1] Sociologically we may characterize this vocation as the construction of a social reality in which members of the family

1. On the notion of "narrative world," of stories making worlds, see the superb statement of Wilder, "Story and Story-World."

may live.[2] Functionally it is creating a communal network of memory and hope in which individual members may locate themselves and discern their identities. But we should note well that such a notion runs deeply counter to the individualism which is valued "on the right" among those who most want the family to recover. Among other things, this view of the family runs counter to the sickness of individualism so pervasive in American ideology.

Family as Alternative Way in the World

In the world of the Old Testament, we may take the family to include the tribe, clan, father's house, all units of social life that consist partly in blood-ties and partly communities of intentional choice and social strategy.[3] In every case the family is a unit that is self-conscious about its life, knowing that work and attention are required to keep the family functioning as a distinct social unit. Such a family knows that it is not an automatic given but only an invitation to construct a social reality of a special kind.

Recent study suggests that "the family" in all these forms functioned in tension with the technically-constructed, bureaucratically-ordered state, city, or city-state. The state or city tended to be ordered in hierarchal and regimented ways. Its functions included the maintenance of order, the administration of justice, and the supervision of production and distribution of goods for the elite to exact as tribute. All of that is, of course, routine, except that such social power claimed and assigned to the city or the state always tends to monopoly; monopoly of force, of goods, of access, so that life is distributed disproportionately, for some at the expense of others. The state or the city as a social force serves to guard and maintain the monopoly.

It may be suggested that what we have called "family"—tribe, clan, father's house—functioned to provide an alternative vision of reality and to practice an alternative way in the world that did not

2. For the clearest statement of the social work of constructing reality, see Berger, *The Sacred Canopy*; and Berger and Luckmann, *The Social Construction of Reality*. Note especially their references to Alfred Schutz.

3. See the careful analysis of Gottwald, *The Tribes of Yahweh*, 237–341. Note his general rubric of family as "protective association."

consent to such monopoly. The more radical form of this notion is that the family provided an alternative way in the world that did not share in the monopolistic tendencies of the dominant structure. The function of the family, in such an understanding, is to nurture folks into an alternative perception of social reality and to practice that social reality in compelling ways. The family then permits and authorizes its members not to participate in the technological enterprise of the large social structure and not to subscribe to its mythology or ideology that justifies and legitimates its technical organizations and policies.[4]

A Counter-Cultural Operation

I have no wish to draw easy analogies or to make simplistic moves from the Bible to our own situation. Perhaps our situation is much more complex than that reflected in the ancient texts. But for a moment consider the sociological crisis of the family in our culture. The overriding social power of our time is what I call *consumer militarism*, which includes the "military-industrial-scientific complex," but which also is sustained by the media, which uncritically fashions images and myths to sustain the dominant value structure. Many of us are domesticated enough so that we understand the family to be a device to nurture folks so that they are suitable and effective participants in the dominant value system. To the extent that the family is to support and enhance the dominant system of technology and ideology, I submit no help can be found in the Bible.

Anyone who has children knows how impressionable they are and is aware of the enormous power of the social realities of the dominant technology and ideology to shape identity, value, worldview in ways that often are not compatible with our Christian notions of social reality. Robert N. Bellah has suggested that the values of this American public reality are ambiguous, containing both good and

4. On the capacity of a unit like the family to dissent from the "Great Story," see the general analysis of Herion, "The Social Organization of Tradition in Monarchic Judah," 51–63 and passim. On the same perspective applied to the contemporary family, see Stanley Hauerwas, *A Community of Character*, 155–74.

bad elements.[5] While this may be true, I submit that in the long run, the articulation of public values sponsored by the dominant complex is inimical to our faith. The most extreme statement known to me of the values now tempting and challenging us, is *Megatrends*,[6] a book that purports to be descriptive but in fact is a vehicle for values that are finally anti-human. In those values one will wait a long time to see or notice anything about human hurt or compassion or human hope. By definition, those matters are simply absent in the new projected world that is coming. I propose that the context of the family in our time, not unlike ancient Israel, is cast in a situation where a social world is readily available, a world of docility, obedience, success, and security. If one reads our situation that way, then the first commandment about "no other gods" is not a discussion about monotheism, but a deep decision about the life-world and social reality to which we give consent and allegiance. I submit that the American family is now facing an issue of the first commandment and is sore pressed with the issue of idolatry as offered in our dominant value system.

The family—which then and now includes tribe, clan, father's house—is an odd and vulnerable counter-force.[7] It does not have available impressive modes of power, either to persuade or coerce. What it does have, however, is *day-to-day access at the crucial nurture points of hurt and amazement.* The social location of the family, I suggest, is not in accommodation to the dominant values, not as a band-aid operation to keep people functioning, but as a daily proposal and glimpse of another way to live in the world. It is not then a privatized or domesticated romantic scene, but it is an area in which deliberate and intentional alternatives are articulated and practiced. I propose then that we understand the family, in light of biblical faith, as a counter-culture operation that finally means to subvert the dominant values. If we do not want our children enmeshed in the

5. Bellah has explored this two sided character of American public reality in various ways and places See especially his programmatic essay, "Civil Religion in America"; and Bellah, *The Broken Covenant.*

6. Cf. Naisbitt, *Megatrends.* My concern is not the *data* Naisbitt presents, but his *casting* of it, which in fact screens out all human questions.

7. Fishbane, *Text and Texture,* 79–83, has shrewdly understood this text as an effort of one generation to transmit its counter-cultural perspective to the next generation He suggests, moreover, that the text hints of the resistance of the new generation to appropriating this alternative perspective.

available values of positivism and technical reason and all they bring with them, then the family is a peculiar chance to construct another world that has more vitality, credibility, and authority in the long run. But it must be a public world, not a private world of escape.

The family, then as now, consists not only in those with blood-ties, but also with ties of intentional choice. That is what the Christian community as family is, a group that has banded together to practice life in an alternative reading.[8]

Memory, Hope, and Obedience

Psalm 78 offers a text for illumination of this notion of the vocation of the family. I suggest it not simply as a text from which to preach, but as a model out of which many other texts can be alternatively understood and interpreted. On this vexed theme, the problem for the preacher is not to find "a good text," but to get clear on the cultural crisis, the theological resources, and the interpretive possibilities. That is, the issues are hermeneutical. I propose Psalm 78 as a way of thinking about those issues. This Psalm is reckoned along with Psalms 105, 106, 136 as an extended recital of Israel's core story, growing out of the credo of texts like Deut 6:20–24; 26:5–9; and Josh 24:1–13.[9] It offers a basic statement of the essentials of Israel's memory.

We may focus on vv. 1–8 which is a call to participate in the recital of memory. In these verses we do not have the substance of the recital, but the *function*. All we know of the substance in these verses is that it is what

> we have heard and known,
>
> > that our fathers have told us. (Ps 78:3)

8. Elliott, *A Home for the Homeless*, has most poignantly discerned the practical dimensions of this alternative reading as it relates to concrete social practice.

9. The basic study of this series of texts is Gerhard von Rad, "The Form Critical Problem of the Hexateuch." See the powerful derivative statement of Walter Harrelson, "Life, Faith and the Emergence of Tradition," with his stress on the "core" tradition. It is that core that is most crucial for the development and maintenance of the family as an alternative reading of reality. I am grateful to Dr. Dorothy Bass for having forcefully called my attention to Psalm 78 in this connection.

In v. 7 we are told the positive function of this story.

1) *It is not to forget the works of God.* Indeed the poem is essentially designed to feed and nurture this memory of acts "from the other side." I submit that the memory of God's works does two things. First, it keeps in awareness the fact that Israel is not *self-made*, is not a self-starter, cannot be self-sufficient, and finally cannot secure its own existence. This was and is an enormous temptation, especially among the competent and the prosperous who forget the real subject of the active verbs and who imagine that "our might and our power have gotten us this wealth" (Deut 8:17). The memory asserts that life begins in inscrutable gift and not in an achievement or a contrivance of ours.

Second, the memory of God's work puts an important past behind the present. In so doing, it deabsolutizes and destabilizes the present. Israel can remember when it was not the way it is now. Moreover, Israel can remember the moment when the present appeared unexpectedly out of the past. Where there is no live memory, Israel is tempted to think it has always been the way it is now (Eccles 1:9–11). If it has always been this way, it must be right and normative. If it is right and normative, then it must be defended at any cost, and certainly not criticized. But with the memory, the present does not need to be so inordinately treasured. The cost of defense can be assessed differently and the present does not need to be beyond criticism. How we engage the present depends largely on what kind of past is set behind it.[10]

2) The recital of the memory is so that they should *set their hope in God* (v. 7). It is odd, but true, that our capacity to hope is precisely correlated with our ability to remember. This Psalm knows that. As memory puts space between past and present, so hope lets us imagine a future that is not just more of the present (cf. Heb 11:1). Notice that in Eccl 1:9–11, it is the loss of memory that leads to the conclusion that there will be nothing new. But this psalm that remembers, is filled with hope. That is because Israel takes its memories and understands them as models for what God will characteristically do in

---

10. See the analysis of Herion, "The Role of Historical Narrative in Biblical Thought," on the very different uses that can be made of memory. See also Smith, *The Memoirs of God.* The relation between memory and current social perception is clearly a reciprocal one.

time to come. The past does not stay past. As Israel remembers that God divided the sea (v. 13), so Israel hopes that God will in the future deliver. The story is told of the past so that the children will know the future is not closed and fated. It is still open to God's powerful resolve that lies beyond the management of the state or the city or any dominant value structure.

3) The recital is done so that Israel *will keep the commandments*. Obedience is a category of health in Israel. Israel is unambiguous. The sovereign God is one who summons and commands and who will be obeyed. This is not a legalistic set of rules. It is not a petty calculation of virtue. It is rather a recognition that life has normative shape which cannot be nullified or circumvented or mocked.

Children of modernity are wont to imagine that all such notions of accountability have been outgrown and superseded as we have "come of age." But, of course, Israel knows better. And we know better. The empire or the state or the city or consumer militarism is not strong enough or true enough to fashion life apart from God's purposes. Soon or late, destruction comes where there is not ready and willing obedience. Such obedience depends on the story being told and heard.

Amnesia, Despair, and Autonomy

Thus v. 7 has a vision of how a world could be constructed, or in our terms, how the family can be organized:

Memory that is rooted in God's acts,

Hope that is aimed at God's new future,

Obedience that heeds God's commands.

The family of Israel is a community resolved to practice *memory, hope,* and *obedience* of a very particular kind. Now those words may be filled with various contents and that requires much conversation among us. But for now we may stay with the large picture. To understand the urgency of these matters, we have paired each one with its opposite, which likely points to the pathology of our time:

Memory . . . or the embrace of *amnesia*.

Hope . . . or the embrace of *despair*.

Obedience . . . or the anxiety of *autonomy*.

Obviously I have moved away from the text, because these negative terms are not present in the text. But, I submit, they are implicit. They announce what it is that the Psalm and the practice of narrative mean to combat. I cite them because I judge them to be a fair statement of our cultural crisis. They articulate what is at issue in the family, and in our culture more generally. They express the odd values which encourage at the same time passionate individualism and intense conformity and I believe we are a society which tries to have both of these at the same time, surely to our destruction.

The argument I make out of the Psalm is that where the family is not telling the story, we may be sure that the next generation (perhaps we are the next generation) becomes a community of amnesia, despair, and autonomy. Where that prevails, everything is possible, everything except life and health. The text states the negative somewhat differently. Where the stories are not told we will become

> a stubborn and rebellious generation,
>
> a generation whose heart was not steadfast
>
> whose spirit was not faithful to God. (Ps 78:8)

Stubborn/rebellious/not steadfast/not faithful: that is a massive indictment that applies not only to religious matters, but to the basic human acts that are essential to family and to society. The Psalm catalogues some of the specifics:

. . . who did not keep covenant (v. 10),

. . . who forget (v. 11),

. . . who sinned more, rebelling (v. 16),

. . . who did not believe (v. 32),

. . . who did not keep in mind his power or his redemption (v. 42).

The psalm tells what happens to this community when it no longer tells the story, no longer knows about memory or hope or obedience. It tries to live without reference or identity and becomes dangerously susceptible to every new ideology. That, I judge, is our situation in which the visible crisis of the family is only a part of a much deeper pathology.

If we translate "rebellion" (v. 8) into amnesia, despair, and autonomy, we are not far from the situation of the contemporary family in our society. We do not refer to immorality, because most of our families are not like that. But it is the case that much family life in our culture has become conformist to the dominant values and dominant rationality without knowing what is happening to us. Rather than maintaining critical distance from the state, the city, the city-state, much family life has become allied with those values. We are, then, in the incongruous situation of embracing as families the very values that finally will destroy the family and prevent the family from doing its humanizing work.

I suggest that the Christian preacher, in recognizing the actual cultural location of the family in American society must consider the family *vis-à-vis* dominant values which are geared to consumerism and militarism which are expressed in conformist ways and which finally will rob us of our humanness. It is clear that if one thinks this way, then the old quarrels about being liberals or conservatives become irrelevant to our real problem.

To the extent that the American family has amnesia,[11] it will conform, because only memory permits critical distance. But when the peculiar memory of hurt and amazement (which is our birthright) is silenced, we will opt for the "big story" told in the empire of success and victory, e.g., a white male reading of American history, the one predominantly taught in our public schools.

To the extent that the American family is in despair, which means having no hope (because there is no memory) we will cling desperately to the way things are. The measure of our despair in public life is that we can think of no viable alternative to militarism. No doubt an index of more intimate despair is the practice of wife abuse and child abuse, actions of desperate people who hope for nothing and so engage in destruction and violence. It could be that military

---

11. On the cultural power of amnesia, see especially the work of Robert J. Lifton. His entire corpus is concerned with this problem, but see especially, *The Broken Connection*, in which he maps the ways in which amnesia is an escape from the historical realities past and present.

adventurism is simply a more respectable form of violence, permitted to those who would never stoop to overt family abuse.

To the extent that the American family is a practitioner of autonomy, serious covenanting communities become impossible. The
notion that the self is the unit of meaning, that we are free to do what
we will, that we need answer to none, that our neighbor is an option
and not a given, all of this creates an illusion of freedom which in fact
is a seductive form of conformity.

My purpose in considering Psalm 78 is both to analyze the pathology that is among us and to suggest a need for a response out of
the tradition. I suggest that the family is under assault, not from the
dangers of drugs and obvious forms of immorality (though these are
true as well as obvious), but the family is under assault from social
ideologies and values that are destructive, so dangerous and destructive because they appear to be compatible with our faith. The first
task of the preacher is to sort out the ways in which these values
challenge and distort our families. Only then is alternative practice
in the family or in the church possible.

To combat these temptations of amnesia, despair, and autonomy; to foster memory, hope and obedience; there is entrusted only
one primary factor . . . *the story.*

This is a very odd, very special, very specific story that belongs
peculiarly to us. We must not be too impressed with "storytelling"
in general, but only with our particular story. To tell this story is not
simply a gesture for entertainment or nostalgia. It is rather a firm,
polemical argument about the shape of our world and our place in
it. The Psalm builds to a stunning conclusion. After long verses on
Israel, it arrives at the judgment (vv. 67–68) that God has at long last
rejected this people and *chosen* an alternative. This is not your normal
romantic theology that is benign and romantic and even-handed.
This story shapes reality to say that life in the world, life with God,
consists in hard choices and decisions. History is a painful process of
rejecting and choosing. Such a notion prevents every excessive certitude. It requires that the danger, openness, and dynamic of covenant
be taken into account. It requires us to recognize that God is not
predictable, controlled, and placed in a box. In this Psalm, *the reject/
choose* notion benefits the David family recently come to power. But
elsewhere, as in the poetry of Amos (Amos 3:2), it is announced that

the chosen people are now the judged people. It is the same freedom of God that amazes and places in jeopardy.

Preaching about the family has nothing to do with maudlin romanticism, or becoming nostalgic. Rather it is an occasion for reflection on the tough issues. Unless the tough issues are joined explicitly and intentionally, Israel always finds itself yet again enmeshed in the dominant values. And that is how it is in the Christian congregation in America. We are deeply enmeshed. We need help sorting out. But the sorting out must not come from fear over some immediate ethical issue. It must come from underneath, where the basic elements of our faith have a chance to present an alternative. The Christian preacher is not engaged in aiding and comforting and relieving our anxiety about the jeopardy we are in. It is rather the task of preaching to help us understand the real jeopardy and to act in liberated and faithful ways. The story gives energy and authority in the face of every controlling system. We may be at a point when the Christian family takes with joy its location of world-making that counters the dominant world that will bring us only death. The family, taken publicly, has a chance for life.

Bibliography

Andersen, Francis I., and David Noel Freedman. *Hosea: A New Translation with Introduction and Commentary.* Anchor Bible 24. Garden City, NY: Doubleday, 1980.

Bellah, Robert N. "Civil Religion in America." *Daedalus* 96 (Winter 1967) 1–21.

———. *The Broken Covenant.* New York: Seabury, 1975.

Berger, Peter L. *The Sacred Canopy: Elements of a Sociological Theory of Religion.* Garden City, NY: Doubleday, 1967.

Berger, Peter L. et.al. *The Homeless Mind: Modernization and Consciousness.* New York: Vintage, 1973.

Berger, Peter L., and Thomas Luckmann, *The Social Construction of Reality.* Garden City, NY: Doubleday, 1966.

Berry, Wendall. *A Place on Earth.* San Francisco: North Point, 1983.

Brodie, Thomas L. *The Elijah–Elisha Narrative as an Interpretive Synthesis of Genesis–Kings and a Literary Model for the Gospels.* Collegeville, MN: Liturgical, 2000.

Brueggemann, Walter. *Divine Presence amid Violence: Contextualizing the Book of Joshua.* Eugene, OR: Cascade Books, 2009.

———. *The Land: Place as Gift, Promise, and Challenge in Biblical Faith.* 2nd ed. Overtures to Biblical Theology. Minneapolis: Fortress, 2002.

———. "Passion and Perspective: Two Dimensions of Education in the Bible." *Theology Today* 42 (1985) 172–80.

———. "Psalm 109: Three Times 'Steadfast Love.'" *Word & World* 5 (1985) 144–54.

———. *Testimony to Otherwise: The Witness of Elijah and Elisha.* St. Louis: Chalice, 2001.

Chaney, Marvin L. "Debt Easement in Israelite History and Tradition." In *The Bible and the Politics of Exegesis: Essays in Honor of Norman K. Gottwald on His Sixty-fifth Birthday*, edited by David Jobling et al., 127–39. Cleveland: Pilgrim, 1991.

Cole, Catherine M. *Performing South Africa's Truth Commission: Stages of Transition.* African Expressive Cultures. Bloomington: Indiana University Press, 2010.

Coote, Robert, editor. *Elijah–Elisha in Socioliterary Perspective.* Semeia Studies. Atlanta: Scholars, 1992.

Crosby, Michael H. *House of Disciples: Church, Economics, and Justice in Matthew.* 1988. Reprinted, Eugene, OR: Wipf & Stock, 2004.

Culley, Robert C. *Studies in the Structure of Hebrew Narratives.* Semeia Supplements 3. Missoula, MT: Scholars, 1976.

Dearman, J. Andrew. *Property Rights in the Eighth-Century Prophets: The Conflict and Its Background.* SBL Dissertation Series 106. Atlanta: Scholars, 1988.

Elliott, John H. *A Home for the Homeless: A Sociological Exegesis of I Peter, Its Situation and Strategy, with a New Introduction.* 1990. Reprinted, Eugene, OR: Wipf & Stock, 2005.

Fishbane, Michael. *Text and Texture.* New York: Schocken, 1979.

Frei, Hans W. *The Eclipse of Biblical Narrative: A Study in Eighteenth and Nineteenth Century Hermeneutics.* New Haven: Yale University Press, 1974.

Frick, Frank S. *The Formation of the State in Ancient Israel.* Social World of Biblical Antiquity Series 4. Sheffield, UK: JSOT Press, 1985.

Fukiyama, Francis. *The End of History and the Last Man.* New York: Free Press, 1992.

Gottwald, Norman K., editor. *Social Scientific Criticism of the Hebrew Bible and Its Social World: The Israelite Monarchy. Semeia* 37 (1986).

———. *The Tribes of Yahweh: A Sociology of the Religion of Liberated Israel, 1250–1050 BCE.* Maryknoll, NY: Orbis, 1979.

Greenberg, Moshe. *Biblical Prose Prayer as a Window to the Popular Religion of Ancient Israel.* Berkeley: University of California Press, 1983.

Guthrie, Harvey H. Jr. *Theology as Thanksgiving; From Israel's Psalms to the Church's Eucharist.* New York: Seabury, 1981.

Harrelson, Walter. "Life, Faith and the Emergence of Tradition." In *Tradition and Theology in the Old Testament,* edited by Douglas A. Knight, 11–31. Philadelphia: Fortress, 1977.

Hauerwas, Stanley. *A Community of Character: Toward a Constructive Christian Social Ethic.* Notre Dame: University of Notre Dame Press, 1981.

Herion, Gary A. "The Role of Historical Narrative in Biblical Thought: The Tendencies Underlying Old Testament Historiography." *Journal for the Study of the Old Testament* 21 (1981) 25–57.

———. "The Social Organization of Tradition in Monarchic Judah." PhD diss., University of Michigan, 1982.

Hiebert, Paula S. "'Whence Shall Help Come to Me?' The Biblical Widow." In *Gender and Difference in Ancient Israel,* edited by Peggy L. Day, 125–41. Minneapolis: Fortress, 1989.

Hillers, Delbert R. *Micah: A Commentary on the Book of the Prophet Micah.* Hermeneia. Philadelphia: Fortress, 1984.

Julian of Norwich. *Showings.* Translated by Edmund Colledge and James Walsh. Classics of Western Spirituality. New York: Paulist, 1978.

Kim, Ee Kon. "'Outcry': Its Context in Biblical Theology." *Interpretation* 42 (1988) 229–39.

Lévinas, Emmanuel. *Totality and Infinity: An Essay on Exteriority*. Translated by Alphonso Lingis. Pittsburgh: Duquesne University Press, 1969.

Lifton, Robert J. *The Broken Connection: On Death and the Continuity of Life*. New York: Simon & Schuster, 1979.

Martyn, J. Louis. *Theological Issues in the Letters of Paul*. Nashville: Abingdon, 1997.

Meeks, M. Douglas. *God the Economist: The Doctrine of God and Political Economy*. Minneapolis: Fortress, 1989.

Miller, Patrick D. *Deuteronomy*. Interpretation. Louisville: Westminster John Knox, 1990.

Miranda, José P. *Marx and the Bible: A Critique of the Philosophy of Oppression*. 1974. Reprinted, Eugene, OR: Wipf & Stock, 2004.

Naisbitt, John. *Megatrends: Ten New Directions Transforming Our Lives*. New York: Warner, 1982.

O'Banion, John D. *Reorienting Rhetoric: The Dialectic of List and Story*. University Park: Pennsylvania State University Press, 1992.

Ozick, Cynthia. *Metaphor and Memory: Essays*. New York: Knopf, 1989.

Premnath, D. N. "Latifundialization and Isaiah 5:8–10." *Journal for the Study of the Old Testament* 40 (1988) 49–60.

Rad, Gerhard von. "The Form Critical Problem of the Hexateuch." In *The Problem of the Hexateuch and Other Essays*, 1–78. Translated by E. W. Trueman Dicken. New York: McGraw Hill, 1966. Reprinted in *From Genesis to Chronicles: Explorations in Old Testament Theology*, 1–58. Translated by E. W. Trueman Dicken. Edited by K. C. Hanson. Fortress Classics in Biblical Studies. Minneapolis: Fortress, 2005.

Smith, Mark S. *The Memoirs of God: History, Memory, and the Experience of the Divine in Ancient Israel*. Minneapolis: Fortress, 2004.

Trible, Phyllis. *God and the Rhetoric of Sexuality*. Overtures to Biblical Theology. Philadelphia: Fortress, 1978.

Tutu, Desmond, and Mpho Tutu. *The Book of Forgiving: The Fourfold Path for Healing Ourselves and Our World*. New York: HarperOne, 2014.

Wallis, Jim. *The Great Awakening: Reviving Faith & Politics in a Post-Religious Right America*. New York: HarperOne, 2008.

Wilder, Amos N. "Story and Story-World." *Interpretation* 37 (1983) 353–64.

Wolff, Hans Walter. *Hosea: A Commentary on the Book of the Prophet Hosea*. Translated by Gary Stansell. Hermeneia. Philadelphia: Fortress, 1974.

———. "Micah the Moreshite—The Prophet and His Background." In *Israelite Wisdom: Theological and Literary Essays in Honor of Samuel Terrien*, edited by John G. Gammie et. al., 77–84. Homage Series 3. Missoula, MT: Scholars, 1978.

A Select Bibliography
of Walter Brueggemann

Embracing the Transformation. Edited by K. C. Hanson. Eugene, OR: Cascade Books, 2013.

Truth Speaks to Power: The Countercultural Nature of Scripture. Louisville: Westminster John Knox, 2013.

Remember You Are Dust. Edited by K. C. Hanson. Eugene, OR: Cascade Books, 2012.

The Practice of Prophetic Imagination: Preaching an Emancipatory Word. Minneapolis: Fortress, 2012.

With Carolyn Sharpe. *Living Countertestimony: Conversations with Walter Brueggemann.* Louisville: Westminster John Knox, 2012.

With Tod Linafelt. *An Introduction to the Old Testament: The Canon and Christian Imagination.* 2nd ed. Louisville: Westminster John Knox, 2012.

Truth-telling as Subversive Obedience. Edited by K. C. Hanson. Eugene, OR: Cascade Books, 2011.

David and His Theologian: Literary, Social, and Theological Investigations of the Early Monarchy. Edited by K. C. Hanson. Eugene, OR: Cascade Books, 2011.

Journey to the Common Good. Louisville: Westminster John Knox, 2010.

Out of Babylon. Nashville: Abingdon, 2010.

Divine Presence amid Violence: Contextualizing the Book of Joshua. Eugene, OR: Cascade Books, 2009.

Great Prayers of the Old Testament. Louisville: Westminster John Knox, 2008.

A Pathway of Interpretation: The Old Testament for Pastors and Students. Eugene, OR: Cascade Books, 2008.

Prayers for a Privileged People. Nashville: Abingdon, 2008.

Praying the Psalms: Engaging Scripture and the Life of the Spirit. 2nd ed. Eugene, OR: Cascade Books, 2007.

The Word Militant: Preaching a Decentering Word. Minneapolis: Fortress, 2007.

The Word that Redescribes the World: The Bible and Discipleship. Edited by Patrick D. Miller. Minneapolis: Fortress, 2006.

The Book that Brings New Life: Scriptural Authority and Biblical Theology. Minneapolis: Fortress, 2004.

Inscribing the Text: Sermons and Prayers of Walter Brueggemann. Edited by Anna Carter Florence. Minneapolis: Fortress, 2004.

Awed to Heaven, Rooted in Earth: Prayers of Walter Brueggemann. Edited by Edwin Searcy. Minneapolis: Fortress, 2003.

Deep Memory, Exuberant Hope: Contested Truth in a Po'st-Christian World. Edited by Patrick D. Miller. Minneapolis: Fortress, 2000.

Texts that Linger, Words that Explode: Listening to Prophetic Voices. Edited by Patrick D. Miller. Minneapolis: Fortress, 2000.

The Covenanted Self: Explorations in Law and Covenant. Edited by Patrick D. Miller. Minneapolis: Fortress, 1999.

Theology of the Old Testament: Testimony, Dispute, Advocacy. Minneapolis: Fortress, 1997.

Index of Scripture

Index of Names